# HOW DO THEY KNOW THEY KNOW?

# HOW DO THEY KNOW THEY KNOW?

## Evaluating Adult Learning

Jane Vella

Paula Berardinelli

Jim Burrow

Jossey-Bass Publishers
San Francisco

Substantial discounts on bulk quantities of Jossey-Bass books are available to corporations, pro-fessional associations, and other organizations. For details and discount information, contact the special sales department at Jossey-Bass Inc., Publishers (415) 433-1740; Fax (800) 605-2665.

For sales outside the United States, please contact your local Simon & Schuster International Office.

Jossey-Bass Web address: http://www.josseybass.com

Manufactured in the United States of America.

**Library of Congress Cataloging-in-Publication Data**

Vella, Jane Kathryn, date
   How do they know they know? : evaluating adult learning / Jane
Vella, Paula Berardinelli, Jim Burrow.—1st ed.
      p.   cm.—(The Jossey-Bass higher and adult education series)
   Includes bibliographcial references (p.   ) and index.
   ISBN 0-7879-1047-3
   1. Adult education—United States.  2. Adult learning—United
States—Evaluation.  3. Popular education—United States.
I. Berardinelli, Paula.  II. Burrow, Jim.  III. Title.  IV. Series.
LC5251.V42   1997
374'.973—dc21                       97–24657

FIRST EDITION
*HB Printing*  10 9 8 7 6 5 4 3 2 1

THE JOSSEY-BASS

HIGHER AND ADULT EDUCATION SERIES

# CONTENTS

# PREFACE

In our work at the Jubilee Popular Education Center we regularly ask, How do they know they know? We believe an accountable response is, Because they did it! This book offers a new approach to the evaluation of adult learning that is congruent with the popular education approach taught in two recent Jossey-Bass publications, *Learning to Listen, Learning to Teach: The Power of Dialogue in Educating Adults* (1994) and *Training Through Dialogue: Promoting Effective Learning and Change with Adults* (1995). In the very short chapter on evaluation in the latter I promised that "my next book will be on the process of evaluation: How can the results of training that uses the popular education approach be effectively and cogently measured?" This book thus advocates a process of accountability, an approach to the evaluation of adult learning we call the *accountability planner*, that narrows the boundaries between planning and evaluation. We do so by evaluating the Introduction to Popular Education course offered by Jubilee Popular Education Center (see Chapter Six) and by examining three diverse programs that use the popular education approach (see Chapter Five).

We stand on the shoulders of those whose work in evaluation over the past fifty years has created a viable and vital field. The approach to evaluation you will learn as you read this book, as we point out in Chapter Two, is deeply rooted in classic evaluation theory, with a special emphasis on accountability and on honoring adult learners as subjects who are decision makers about their learning. If you have read *Learning to Listen, Learning to Teach* and *Training Through Dialogue*, you have a clear sense of what we mean by popular education. If you have not, here is a summary.

## Popular Education

In Latin America certain churches and health groups, following the seminal work of Brazilian educator Paulo Freire, began to design their educational work with communities as a dialogue. They called this *educación popular* to distinguish it from traditional schoolroom education and traditional adult education. In other parts of the world this is called *nonformal education*. By whatever name, it is characterized by certain transcultural traditions:

- *Participation* of the learners in determining what is to be learned through needs assessment
- *Dialogue* between learner and teacher and among learners
- *Small-group work* to engage learners
- *Visual support* and *psychomotor involvement*
- *Accountability:* "How do they know they know?"
- *Participative feedback* on results of programs
- *Respect* for learners and teachers
- A *listening attitude* on the part of teachers and resource people
- Learners *do* what they are learning

As you can see, popular education is no different from traditional adult education except that it demands congruence between theory and practice. At the Jubilee Popular Education Center we say, because we must, that in our Introduction to Popular Education course we will do what we are teaching.

Jubilee Popular Education Center was opened in 1981 to teach adult educators how to incorporate aspects of popular education into their own courses and materials. It is called "Jubilee" because the center celebrates learning. We now have more than 800 Jubilee Fellows who have completed the Introduction to Popular Education course. They are adult educators in the fields of medicine, health promotion, nursing, literacy, human resource development, sociology, theology, and social work; they are university professors, field workers in nonprofit groups, doctors in clinics and hospitals, teachers in public school systems, trainers in industry, and consultants. Thirty Jubilee Associates are now master trainers who can and do teach the Introduction to Popular Education course in English, Spanish, French and Portuguese. This is the basic course examined in Chapter Six. The center has a curriculum of courses that now includes a five-day course on the evaluation of adult learning. We teach the fifty principles and practices of popular education (Vella, 1995) and seven steps of planning that we believe are basic to the design of accountable learning.

We wrote this book because we see a need for a process of evaluating adult learning that is congruent with the principles and practices of popular education, a process that honors the designer-evaluator as the subject or decision maker just as the popular education approach honors learners as subjects: decision makers about their own learning. Evaluation in this accountability process is seen as a partnership, a means of ongoing autonomous praxis—that is, a highly structured and organic part of the entire design. Jim Burrow and Paula Berardinelli have worked in the field of educational program design and evaluation for years. They bring a wealth of technical knowledge and years of research. My part in this team is to make sure that what we present of their practical and profound insights is accessible to practicing adult educators, such as the readers of *Learning to Listen, Learning to Teach* and *Training Through Dialogue*. My colleagues acknowledge that their technical contributions have to pass the "Jane Test."

We three authors have gained privileged insights into the power of the principles of popular education and the process of accountability through the writing of this book, which was a research agenda from the start, where questions were formed, examined, and answered by us as a team. All the principles and practices of popular education described in *Training Through Dialogue* were manifest throughout our work together. We discovered some new principles at work: Jim's humility in constantly celebrating what he has learned from me and Paula; Paula's congruence, demonstrated by constantly checking how the evaluation process uses the theories of adult learning; and my use of stories, constantly relating abstract concepts to real-life situations. We used the seven steps of planning not only as part of the content of the book but also in planning its design: *Who* is this book for? *Why* do these readers need it? *When* will it be useful? *Where* can it find and serve them? *What* content is essential? *What* can they look forward to doing (in other words, what should be their achievement-based objectives) after they finish reading the book? And finally, *how* should we organize and compose the book?

## Who Will Find this Book Useful?

We trust that all who have been excited and moved by the popular education approach described in *Learning to Listen, Learning to Teach* and *Training Through Dialogue* will open this book with trust, anticipating that they will gain solid learning about how to evaluate popular education programs. The many Jubilee Fellows and Associates who have worked to develop skills in this approach to popular education can examine what they find here with a glint of recognition, having heard much of it in the courses they took with Jubilee. They are waiting for this book, knowing that the choice is theirs as to how they use this evaluation process in their educational programs. They will especially enjoy Chapter Four, which explains how to design evaluation instruments for their existing programs.

Community education groups may see themselves in the NETWORK case study in Chapter Five; NETWORK is a social justice lobby in Washington, D.C. The University of Washington case study may be used by schools of public health, medicine, and nursing that are teaching health education. They can examine how they are processing a popular education approach to the clinical and community work of health educators. Professors of adult education who specialize in evaluation can use this book as a text that can lead them toward an accountable, cogent alternative approach to program planning and evaluation. Not-for-profit organizations may see themselves in the example of Literacy Volunteers of America, where they say the popular education approach has "changed the way we work." As readers decide how to use this process of accountability they will develop a sound response to the question posed by the book's title: How do they know they know?

We are developing a software package and other supporting resources that will make this approach even more accessible to practicing adult educators and trainers. To discover the status of that development and to get information on all the courses in the curriculum, please contact Jubilee Popular Education Center, Inc., at 1221 Moultrie Court, Raleigh, North Carolina 27615. The e-mail address is jubileenc@aol.com, and the phone numbers are (919) 847–3804; 1 (800) 639–8138; fax (919) 870–0599.

## Overview of the Contents

This book has seven chapters. Chapter One shows how Jubilee has developed from a rudimentary conceptualization and practice of evaluation to a more intentional process as a result of the research on this book. You will find a new learning needs assessment tool to enable learners to gather their own baseline data. Chapter Two gives an overview of evaluation, connecting the key principles to classic theory from Tyler to Guba. The genesis of the accountability process and the theory of impact is also described. Chapter Three describes the accountability process further, offering what we call the accountability planner as an instrument to use in planning and evaluating an educational program. By the end of Chapter Three you should have a good sense of this accountability process as a guide to planning and evaluation.

Chapter Four explains how to select those components of the accountability process that will fit the context and configuration of the program you want to evaluate. We know that most readers will be working in programs already in place that need evaluation from either internal sources (clients, staff, board) or external sources (funding agencies, regional or state associations). We have seen that the best use of this approach is the most autonomous use, so the challenge is put to you: What aspect of this process will be most useful in your existing program? In Chapter Five we use the accountability process to evaluate the impact of the Jubilee approach to popular education in three instances: first, on training materials being used by NETWORK throughout the United States; second, on a course on health education being taught in the Graduate School of Public Health at the University of Washington in Seattle; and third, on the entire organization of Literacy Volunteers of America (LVA) as discerned through its new popular education approach to training throughout the organization. Each case study describes the situation, offers a synopsis of the program, shows the accountability planner as used by the case group, offers an analysis of the data produced by using that accountability planner, and makes a final synthesis. Note that we move from an examination of a program that is evaluating materials (NETWORK) to a program that can evaluate the materials, process, and impact (the University of Washington) to a program that is working on a macro level within an organization (LVA). In Chapter Six we demonstrate how this process of accountability works in Jubilee. As we use the accountability planner in the redesign of the Introduction to Popular Education course you can project how it might be useful in your planning for accountable learning. You will see how the technical language of evaluation can be simplified and put to work. Just as the principles and practices of popular education demand time up front in preparation, so does the use of this accountability process demand hard work during planning to anticipate changes, name indicators or evidence of success, and describe necessary documentation. The struggle is shown in Chapter Six.

In Chapter Seven we offer our reflections on all this, including final notes on the who, why, and what of evaluation. We offer some new assumptions and deductions about program evaluation of popular education. Finally, we speak to future uses of this theory and practice: What are our next steps? We include a narrative glossary of education, planning, and evaluation terms used in this book and other terms related to popular education. Throughout the book, in sections entitled "Your Turn," we invite the reader to consider ways to use the theory or practice you are reading about on your own programs.

More than anything else we want this book to be accessible. Recently, I attended a lecture at a nearby university on the evaluation of a health education program. The lecturer described a $60 million pilot project on AIDS education that, she admitted, spent the majority of those dollars on evaluation of the program! In the darkened classroom, she used an overhead projector to show a set of diagrams and charts showing the evaluation results. She had to admit that the numbers were too complex to be used by health educators and policy makers to determine either the impact or the future of the program. An esoteric set of graphs and equations showed the results of the six-year program; the evaluation may have been valid and quantifiable, but it was not accessible.

Even more recently I was part of a management training program. Eighty program managers came together for a four-day retreat. In their replies to a needs assessment survey they offered sound reasons for coming, but the evaluation report, designed by a separate team, never referred to the needs assessment data. Instead the evaluation invited subjective feedback and a quantitative analysis of responses to five subjective closed questions, such as this one:

The presenter exhibited a thorough understanding of the topic.

Not at all          1          2          3          4          5          Very well

In the end, the evaluation data did not tell with any authority what had been learned, what impact the learning had, or what changes were necessary in the design of future programs. In other words, the evaluation was not valid even though the data were accessible. We propose a system that is both valid and accessible, that is accountable to learner and teacher alike.

This book assumes the desire of readers to use an adult education approach to adult learning that is based on mutual respect, honors the learners as the subjects of their own learning, and trusts in the power of human beings to work together and communicate in honest dialogue. Therefore we have held ourselves accountable to present in accessible language an evaluation process congruent to such a learning process. My experience has proven time and time again that men and women will use their natural powers when they have a say in the design and evaluation of the processes that evoke their learning. This is the heart of the accountability process demonstrated here. Learners are accountable first to themselves. The accountability planner in this process of evaluation allows us to be accountable to the learners and to the wider community that will be affected by their learning.

This book would never be available to readers without the assiduous work of Gale Erlandson and her team at Jossey-Bass, including their professional readers who offered such helpful and clear suggestions for making the manuscript accessible to all.

My thanks to my colleagues Jim Burrow and Paula Berardinelli, who brought humor and wisdom to this enterprise. You will come to appreciate them as I do as you read the book. Please keep this important research agenda going and growing by sharing your discoveries about evaluation with Jubilee. We welcome your partnership and your continued collaboration.

*September 1997*                                                        Jane Vella
*Raleigh, North Carolina*

# THE AUTHORS

JANE VELLA is president of Jubilee Popular Education Center in Raleigh, North Carolina. She is the author of *Learning to Listen, Learning to Teach: The Power of Dialogue in Educating Adults* (1994) and *Training Through Dialogue: Promoting Effective Learning and Change with Adults* (1995), both published by Jossey-Bass. She received her bachelor of arts degree in 1955 from Rogers College in New York, her master of arts degree from Fordham University in 1965, and her doctorate in adult education from the University of Massachusetts at Amherst. Vella taught at North Carolina State University and is an adjunct professor at the School of Public Health of the University of North Carolina at Chapel Hill. Vella has worked in community education and training since 1953 in more than forty countries.

PAULA BERARDINELLI has been a student of Jane Vella and of Jubilee Popular Education since 1989. Berardinelli studied at Pennsylvania State University and then collaborated with Jim Burrow on the creation of the Accountability Process and Planner that began with her dissertation research at North Carolina State University on the impact of training. She founded the Center for Organizational Research and Education (CORE) in Raleigh, North Carolina, and has taught undergraduate and graduate courses at North Carolina State University. As a consultant to business and industry Berardinelli has successfully used the principles and practices of popular education; at present she is collaborating on the development of an electronic version of the theory of impact, including an interactive accountability planner.

JIM BURROW has both academic preparation and experience in the worlds of business and education. With an undergraduate degree in marketing from the University of Northern Iowa and graduate degrees in marketing education from that school and the University of Nebraska, Burrow has spent the past twenty-five years teaching at the community college and university levels as well as designing and delivering training programs and consulting in business and industry. He is coauthor of several textbooks, most recently *Marketing Foundations and Functions* with Steven A. Eggland. For the past eight years Burrow has focused on human resource development and training with particular attention to performance-based training in industry. As a part of that work, he has collaborated with Paula Berardinelli in studying systems to improve the transfer of training from the classroom to the workplace and to measure the impact of training on organizational outcomes. Burrow is currently consulting with several Fortune 500 companies on improving their training effectiveness using systematic evaluation. He is currently associate professor and coordinator of the graduate training and development program in the Department of Adult and Community College Education of North Carolina State University at Raleigh, North Carolina.

# HOW DO THEY KNOW THEY KNOW?

CHAPTER ONE

# A NEW WAY OF THINKING ABOUT EVALUATION

*Nothing is as practical as a good theory.*

KURT LEWIN

I n this chapter we shall see the connection between this book and two other Jossey-Bass publications, *Learning to Listen, Learning to Teach: The Power of Dialogue in Educating Adults* (1994) and *Training Through Dialogue: Promoting Effective Learning and Change with Adults* (1995), both of which present a specific approach to adult education. The theoretical base of the approach taught in those books is eclectic: Kurt Lewin's field theory of motivation, Paulo Freire's theory of problem posing, and Malcolm Knowles's andragogy, to name a few. Jubilee Popular Education Center in Raleigh, North Carolina, has been doing research on this approach since 1981. The research included endless questions about evaluation processes and resulted in this collaboration with specialists who had designed a theory of impact (Berardinelli, 1991). We examine that model generally in Chapters Two and Three, but this book focuses overall on one part of it: the accountability process to evaluate adult learning. This is a planning and evaluation process that respects the learner, is specific and clear about sequence, engages the learner from the beginning in response and analysis, and in fact uses all the principles and practices of popular education (Vella, 1995).

It has always been important in Jubilee courses to have learners self-evaluate, as subjects or decision makers of their own learning. Evaluation is a means of celebrating obvious learning and of getting feedback on perceived gaps between what we said we would do and what actually happened for the learner. The learner's voice has always been central to evaluation in both immediate feedback and long-term (longitudinal) responses.

Following are two sets of theory in practice. The first is labeled "before" and describes how Jubilee thought about and taught about evaluation before the development of this book; the second is labeled "after" and explains Jubilee's current beliefs about evaluation as a function of the theory developed and described in the book. Perhaps the change you see in our theoretical construct and practice will encourage you. The construct on evaluation is in two parts: how we get baseline data for evaluation (that is, how we assess learning needs and resources), and what and how we teach about planning and evaluation.

## Before

The idea of educators and trainers opening a dialogue with learners prior to the course or workshop session is most compelling to participants in Jubilee courses. They are often shocked when staff telephone them before they come to the course to talk about the expectations they share in their learning needs and resources assessment survey. They consistently say that doing a needs assessment before they design and teach within the Introduction to Popular Education course is a revelation to them. We have always said that the dialogue with learners should begin long before the course does. So we faithfully did a survey needs assessment prior to the course, talking to a sample of the participants, perhaps five out of ten, for a few minutes to review their needs and resources assessment survey response and to ask their concerns about the course.

### Getting Baseline Data

The learning needs assessment instrument Jubilee used prior to our writing this book was a simple set of open-ended questions; see Exhibit 1.1.

Doing such a needs assessment was as much a part of the processing of the popular education approach as it was a means to discover specific and useful baseline data. The questions were general in order to be safe for the learner. The data received were informative, not operative; that is, they did not change any of our intentions, achievement-based objectives, or learning tasks. They did not specify exactly where learners were headed with the new skills, knowledge, and attitudes they developed in the course. We thought we were doing very well with this system. We had much to learn.

### Teaching Evaluation Theory and Practice

To teach evaluation theory and practice in the Jubilee Master Trainer course, we used the learning tasks shown in Exhibit 1.2.

These learning tasks show that we at Jubilee were clear in theory and practice about the distinction between immediate evaluation (sometimes called feed-

## EXHIBIT 1.1. JUBILEE'S LEARNING NEEDS ASSESSMENT: BEFORE.

### Learning Needs Assessment Survey

Name

Present work situation

1. You have read the achievement-based objectives for this course in the original packet. Describe your present work situation and tell how you see yourself using the skills, knowledge, and attitudes you will develop during this course.
2. Which of these program objectives seem most relevant to you in your present situation?
3. What are some of the common problems you face when designing courses and teaching adults?
4. What have you read recently that was helpful to you in your work in adult education?

Please send your responses to these questions to Jubilee by _____ .

May we talk by phone with you during the week of _____ to review what you have written here?

If yes, day to call _____ Time _____ Number to call _____ .

                                                            Thank you!

---

back) and long-term (longitudinal) evaluation. We recognized and taught quite clearly the distinction between qualitative data and quantitative data. However, the problem we now perceive is that these learning tasks on evaluation are too general; they do not hold the learner or teacher accountable and do not result in hard data to confirm results or to use in making changes in a course after it has been evaluated. What the learners perceive as they respond to the evaluation questions is one thing; what they are actually doing differently as a result of the learning is another.

In the current literature on evaluation, the concept of utilization is dominant. How can you measure the learner's continuing use of a new skill, new concept, or newly developed attitude? That is the operative question of today's evaluators. We did recognize that measuring utilization within the course (immediate evaluation) is far different from measuring it after the course (longitudinal evaluation); we simply did not have a theory or process for measuring specific utilization before preparing this book.

Notice that the learning tasks do not mention baseline data nor make any reference to how they can be used in measuring progress or impact. It is not enough to gather information about adult learners and their needs and desires for learning; one must have a process for using such data. The purpose here is to get data

## EXHIBIT 1.2. JUBILEE MASTER COURSE'S
## EVALUATION LEARNING TASKS: BEFORE.

### Evaluation Learning Task

This task has four content topics:
A. 1. Immediate evaluation
   2. Longitudinal evaluation
B. 1. Qualitative evaluation
   2. Quantitative evaluation

A. 1. *Immediate evaluation* usually involves an initial response: an affective response and some measures denoting immediate usefulness of what was learned.

   Learning task: Examine this first example of tasks for immediate evaluation of this Master Trainer course.

   a. Examine the achievement-based objectives of this course found on page 3. Which of these did you achieve? How well? Which of these do you feel needs more work?
   b. Describe the high point of the course for you so far—the point when you felt yourself learning.
   c. Name the changes you recommend Jubilee make in the next course (program, content, logistics, site, what else?).

2. *Long-term or longitudinal evaluation* is done after a definite period of time to examine behavior change. It often invites response to the original design.

   Learning task: Examine this example of long-term or longitudinal evaluation.

   Dear _____ ,

   a. It has been six months since you took the course Introduction to Popular Education. Please indicate in what ways your planning, materials design, and teaching have changed in the past six months.
   b. If you had the chance, which of these selected content topics included in the course would you want to study further? Please check them here:
      ☐ Adult learning theory
      ☐ Problem-posing approach: dialogue
      ☐ The "banking" approach: monologue
      ☐ Lewin's dozen principles for learning
      ☐ Respect; the use of lavish affirmation
      ☐ Achievement-based objectives
      ☐ Subject: the learner as decision maker, never as an object to be used
   c. What would you add to this long-term (longitudinal) evaluation?

B. 1. *Qualitative evaluation* uses indicators that relate to changes in specific behaviors, attitudes, and skill levels as perceived by the learners themselves, by those who work with them, and by the educators. For example, a Jubilee Fellow sends colleagues and friends to the next course; a Jubilee Fellow sends designs to Jubilee for reflection and suggestions; and a Jubilee Fellow inquires about further readings in any sector.

   Learning task: Name other indicators of qualitative evaluation for the introductory course.

2. *Quantitative evaluation* offers numerical indicators of changes in behavior and attitudes. For example, a Jubilee Fellow orders *ten* copies of the book for her colleagues at work, a Jubilee Fellow uses the seven steps of planning *each time* she designs a program, a Jubilee Fellow sends *six* colleagues to the course; a Jubilee Fellow gets a *10 percent* raise for creative work within a year, and a Jubilee Fellow wins a *$100,000* grant for training for her company.

   Learning task: What would you add to these quantitative measures of achievement?

in advance so we can help learners track progress as they work through the course and as they try to utilize their new knowledge afterward.

For example, a company could send a secretary to an expensive course entitled How to Use the Latest Word Processing Program. Both at the end of the course and back at work, the secretary may show efficient use of the skills taught. But without baseline data no one could tell if this was progress; perhaps the individual was skilled in the use of the program before beginning the course. This front-loaded process of soliciting and examining baseline data for what it tells about the learner and about the appropriateness of the curriculum is demanding, and it demonstrates our point: the dialogue should begin in earnest long before the course begins!

Until now Jubilee has not presented to its Fellows a system for efficient and compelling evaluation that affects not only the measurement of learning, transfer, and impact but, more important, the planning and design of any course in terms of anticipated results. Now we have a systematic use of sound principles and practices of evaluation. It will be reviewed in Chapter Two, described in detail in Chapter Three, and reviewed again in Chapter Seven. These principles and practices make a difference in the accountability of adult education courses that reflect concern about quality adult learning and that therefore use the popular education approach.

Before doing the research and collaborative writing of this book we were where many educators still seem to be: wanting to do participative planning and evaluation, aware of how vital it is in shaping relevant curriculum, but unskilled in designing cogent evaluation questions and getting specific needs assessment data. As already stated, we thought we were teaching well about evaluation processes, but we had much to learn. We hope this book will be one step for all of us toward developing a workable theory and a reasonable practice of accountable evaluation that is useful for learners and teachers alike.

## After

Today at Jubilee there is a new sense of precision and order in the air. The learning needs assessment for the Introduction to Popular Education course is now done very differently from how it was described in *Training Through Dialogue* (Vella, 1995, pp. 113–114).

### Getting Baseline Data

The material we now send out to participants when they register for the course is shown in Exhibit 1.3.

## EXHIBIT 1.3.  JUBILEE'S LEARNING NEEDS ASSESSMENT: NOW.

### Needs Assessment Process

Dear _____ ,

This course, Learning to Listen, Learning to Teach: An Introduction to Popular Education, is at once a study in epistemology and the practice of a dynamic approach to adult learning. The core value at Jubilee is that the adult learners are subjects or decision makers about their own learning. As you prepare to take the course, consider using four approaches to getting valid baseline data on your present skills, knowledge, and attitudes:

1. *Picture:* invite a colleague to videotape you teaching a course, leading a meeting, making a presentation, or giving a lecture. A half-hour videotape can be rich data. During the course, your practice teaching or presentation will be videotaped. This will give you an opportunity for useful comparison.
2. *Preparation:* collect evidence of how you prepare for a presentation, lecture, course, or meeting. What guidelines do you usually use? What are the steps in your preparation?
3. *Program:* find a program plan for one of your recent presentations, courses, lectures, or meetings. Do not alter it; present it as you did it so you can compare it to a program you design after this course.
4. *Perception*: Invite a student from a course or a lecture, or a colleague who attended a meeting or sat through a recent presentation you did, to write a one-page response to two questions:
   - What do you perceive are the strengths of _____ as demonstrated by this experience?
   - What aspects would you like to see him or her work on and improve?

Your response to this preparatory process is really the first learning task of the course. The optimal response is one that uses all four elements: picture, preparation, program plan, and perception. Bring these materials to the course. You will use them to judge the changes that take place in your skills, knowledge, and attitudes throughout the week.

Your response to this learning needs assessment is entirely determined by you according to your context. This needs assessment is structured to provide a thorough analysis of your *present* knowledge and skills. This will provide baseline data for you to use to compare where you are now and where you are at the end of the course. This is for your personal celebration of learning and growth. Throughout this experience you will be building your Jubilee portfolio. It will include

- A first half-hour video tape dated _____ (picture)
- Planning steps paper (see item 2 above; preparation)
- Plan or design paper (see item 3 above; program)
- Letter from one person in response to your two-question survey (perception)
- A copy of the survey [see Exhibit 1.1] response you sent to Jubilee.

Thank you!

The achievement-based objectives mentioned in the first survey question are shown in detail in Chapter Six and in the Appendix. This new needs assessment process gives learners hard baseline data so they can measure their own progress. As they compare their first videotape of teaching with the two developed in the course, they see exactly what they have learned and how their behavior has changed. As they examine how they prepared for a session before the course and compare it with their new designs afterward, they can celebrate their learning. How do they know they know? Because they just did it.

The Jubilee Associates leading the course review this data before beginning to teach for many reasons: to get a profile of the learners, to see their learning needs, to anticipate where in the course these needs can best be met, and to begin the dialogue with the learners long before the course begins. It is important to recognize that the needs assessment data do not form the course but rather inform it. It is up to the educators to make final decisions on the content of the course, the *what* in the seven steps of planning (see the Preface for a review of these). That content is then taught through an accountable process that meets the now explicit needs of this group of learners.

## Teaching Evaluation Theory and Practice

Teaching and designing all the courses in the Jubilee curriculum—the Introduction to Popular Education course, the Advanced course, the Master Trainer course, and the new Evaluation First course—are different now because of the new precision and order. As you will read about in Chapter Six, we have examined our content and achievement-based objectives using the accountability process and the accountability planner. We discovered, for example, that we needed to add a content piece on how to use a video clip. The reason is that we had an achievement-based objective stating that "participants will have examined the use of a video clip," but no lesson on how to use a video clip in the description of our course's content. The accountability planner helped us discover that incongruity in design.

Thinking of evaluation this way forces us to be more intentional and therefore more accountable to the learners. At the end of the course, we can point to all the specific content pieces—skills, knowledge, attitudes, and referring to the achievement-based objectives and the parallel learning tasks—to remind participants that they have indeed achieved what we promised they would. The quality of their achievement is idiosyncratic and will be measured against their future utilization of the learning (longitudinal indicators) as well as against their work within the course (immediate indicators).

At Jubilee we offer a money-back guarantee: if you have not learned what you came to learn by the end of the week, you get your money back. We have not yet had a request for a refund. Now, however, we are more certain that such a request would be an anomaly because the design is more fully accountable. This kind of evaluation is demanding. We at Jubilee had to make a personal paradigm shift equivalent to the one we invite people to make when they first attempt to use the popular education approach. It is neither comfortable nor easy to make such a shift. However, the value of this more complete picture is compelling. We know our teaching and the materials we produce to teach with will be more precise, more relevant to the particular learners, more accessible, and, above all, more accountable. That is where we are now in this development of a new theory and process of evaluation.

### *YOUR TURN*

We have described where we were at Jubilee before our new research on evaluation. Describe where you are now in your perception of evaluation. How do you presently do evaluation in your own work? How does your planning relate to the evaluation process? How do you discover learning needs? What did you learn about yourself as an educator as you read this chapter? What do you hope to learn as you examine the accountability process and apply it to your teaching situations? This informal reflective survey can offer you baseline data that can be a touchstone for you as you move through the rest of the book.

CHAPTER TWO

# BUILDING FROM THE BASE

## Philosophy and Practice

In this chapter we begin our journey toward effective evaluation. We think it is important that you, the reader, understand the philosophy of evaluation we bring to this book as well as some of the basic principles we believe guide effective evaluation. In our discussion with many people who are responsible for planning and managing education and training programs, we often hear words of anxiety and apprehension about evaluation. The cause in many cases appears to be externally imposed evaluation systems that seem complex and time-consuming or largely irrelevant to the program's purpose or outcomes. In other conversations we hear concern that educators and trainers do not feel competent to plan evaluations or analyze and interpret data. Their experiences with evaluation texts or presentations by evaluators have left them with the belief that they cannot design evaluations that meet the expectations of "experts."

We begin by explaining that evaluation strategies can be quite different from organization to organization and that no one system is better than all others. We then examine characteristics of effective evaluation and share some of our philosophy in a section on what we call evaluation axioms. Finally, we introduce you to the evaluation process developed by Paula Berardinelli and Jim Burrow, the theory of impact (1991), which provides the foundation for this book. We share with you the ideas and the people who have been instrumental in shaping our experience with and beliefs about evaluation.

### *YOUR TURN*

Before you begin, take a few minutes to think about your experience with and attitudes toward evaluation.

- If you currently view evaluation as an important part of each program for which you are responsible, how does that show in the process as you evaluate?
- What key elements of a philosophy of evaluation that guide your efforts can you articulate?
- As a practicing adult educator, when do you feel that you have the autonomy to design evaluation in such a way that it helps you improve the education process as well as the results of the program?

## Evaluation by Design

*Evaluation.* Maybe no word generates as much feeling in education. Do any of the following scenarios reflect your feelings?

- Students sit at their desks in a classroom with looks of either confidence or terror on their faces depending on how well prepared they are for the upcoming exam and how successful they have been on tests in the past.
- A letter arrives from a funding agency informing the program coordinator that an evaluation team is scheduled for a two-day visit next month.
- The members of a planning team and the instructors gather after an exhaustive effort to design and deliver a training program to ask, "Did we make a difference?"

Almost all planning models used in education and training include an evaluation component. Yet often the least amount of time is devoted to preparing educators to incorporate evaluation effectively into their programs. Without adequate preparation, educators bring only their past experiences and personal perceptions to their understanding of evaluation. As a result, evaluation can be misunderstood, misinterpreted, misused, or even ignored by many.

Yes, evaluation can be a formal test as perceived by the students in a classroom, but it does not have to be a terrifying experience. Indeed, evaluation is often demanded by funding agencies but does not have to be completed only through a one-time visit by an outside team of experts. And, of course, evaluation should be a concern of all program planners and instructors. It does not have to be considered only at the end of the program, however. A more comprehensive view of evaluation opens possibilities and potential and alleviates concerns and misunderstandings.

## An Analogue for Evaluation: Planning a Journey

Few people are comfortable starting a long journey without planning. Some spend painstaking hours considering alternatives, charting routes, and developing and printing schedules and budgets. Others are more general in their plans, setting broad parameters for the trip and remaining flexible to change the itinerary as they go. In each case, however, goals and checkpoints are developed to guide the journey. They may be as specific as a detailed map, an hour-by-hour itinerary for each day, and a specific budget allocating amounts to be spent for travel, lodging, meals, and other anticipated expenses. Or they may be as general as an overall plan for a week's travel identifying likely destinations, possible activities, and a maximum amount of money to spend, with the prospect of making changes as the journey goes on. In either case the checkpoints make it possible to determine whether the journey is progressing in a way that meets the needs of the planners as well as of any others who are along.

Consider the nature of those checkpoints. On a carefully prepared road map for a trip by automobile, routes are marked to identify the highways to be followed and the major towns or cities to be passed along the way. As the journey progresses, the navigator studies the map to ensure that the correct turns are made, that highway signs match the route numbers on the map, and that each city passed is the one identified on it. If the checkpoint is a budget, someone will track expenditures and match them with the amount budgeted. If the cost of a motel room exceeds the budget, a second choice must be found or the budget revised to accommodate the higher expense. Savings on meals one day may allow an extra treat another day.

Even the person using a general plan will set some checkpoints; if an extra day is spent at one city or attraction, for example, a decision must be made to shorten or eliminate the time spent at another location in order to end the trip on schedule. With only a maximum amount of money to spend rather than a detailed budget, the traveler must keep an eye on the remaining funds so as not to run out before making it back home.

Evaluation can be likened to these two types of trip planning. Some people choose the more specific and prescriptive "road maps" and "budgets" that can be checked carefully and frequently to ensure that an educational program is progressing toward its outcomes. Others rely on more general evidence of direction, which allows a great deal of flexibility in the program while still directing it toward a planned result. In each case, some type of plan and checkpoints must be identified before the program begins. Otherwise, just as travelers without a plan will never know if they have reached their destination, educators without plans and checkpoints will be uncertain if they have met expectations.

### A Means Rather Than an End

The narrow view of evaluation is that it is the ending point of a learning experience. After completing an activity or a program, we evaluate it to determine whether it brought about change, and if so whether it was the change we anticipated. But the result of such evaluation is limited to either "yes, we were effective" or "no, we were not"; little is possible beyond a general feeling of accomplishment or disappointment. The broader view of evaluation is that it is an integral part of a learning experience—as important at the beginning and throughout the experience as it is at the end. With this view, evaluation becomes a tool for continual improvement; it is part of the education program, helping ensure the success of the learning experience through ongoing feedback rather than relying simply on making an ending judgment.

## Characteristics of Effective Evaluation

We suggest that there are several characteristics of effective evaluation:

1. It must be objective. Evaluation designed to make a program look good serves little purpose; instead, it should provide clear evidence to indicate whether a program is leading to desired change.
2. It should identify the important elements of an educational program. Educators, using professional judgment, make specific decisions about learning experiences they believe will lead to the desired result; evaluation of the program elements helps improve one's professional judgment for future planning.
3. Evaluation should match the organizational philosophy. Organizations determine their own purpose and use of evaluation; what is useful to one may have little meaning or value to another. Imposing an evaluation plan without an understanding of the purpose or mission of an organization will likely result in harmful or ignored results.
4. Evaluation measures should be identifiable and accessible. Often the reason cited for failure to evaluate is that the process is too difficult and time-consuming. Thus evaluations should be designed such that they can be conducted within the structure and resources of the educational program by the people responsible for it. They should not impose significant burdens on either the learners or the organization.
5. Evaluation should focus on both the outcomes and the process. Two critical questions guide evaluation: "Did we accomplish our objectives?" and "Did we accomplish them in an effective and efficient way?" Evaluation can and should provide answers to both.

## Evaluation Axioms

Evaluation axioms provide the foundation for our philosophy of evaluation. They set a tone for how we believe evaluation should be approached as a part of an educational program. Following are our evaluation axioms.

*Evaluation does not just happen.* Do you believe you can judge whether a program was successful or not by your feelings at the end of a program? Such feelings may contribute to an overall evaluation, but they are clearly subjective and often shaped by the moment. Evaluation should be carefully designed just as the educational program is thoughtfully planned; and just as an effective educational experience is not haphazard, evaluation will not occur unless carefully planned and managed.

*Evaluation must be done by experts.* A frequent evaluation error is seeking evidence of effectiveness from people who are not qualified to judge. Although learners can tell us whether a particular experience was interesting or satisfying, they are usually not qualified to judge such factors as the subject matter expertise of the instructor, or even their own ability to apply what they have learned after they return to their job. Judgments about the subject matter expertise of an instructor are made best by people who are themselves expert in the subject area; learners are better able to identify whether the instructor was able to communicate the information in an understandable way. Learners can describe whether they have the confidence to attempt to apply what they have learned, but judgments about their future effectiveness are best made by a supervisor or an experienced colleague through observing the learners after their return to the organization.

*Effective evaluation returns more than it costs.* Evaluation results should add value to the organization, so before evaluation the organization must determine what information is needed and how it will be used. Otherwise evaluation plans will not have a clear focus and may be either inadequate or more extensive than needed. Without adequate evaluation, potential program improvements will go unrecognized; overevaluation will often hide important information or overwhelm and discourage decision makers.

*Evaluation can be accomplished in many ways.* A large number of evaluation tools are available to make judgments about an educational program. Tools can be selected that fit an evaluation philosophy, a particular program design, the time and resources of the organization, and the skills and interests of the educators and learners. Careful selections need to be made to ensure that the tools are appropriate and do not limit or interfere with the program. In the next section we examine some of the factors that can guide you in selecting evaluation tools.

### *YOUR TURN*

There is, indeed, no one accepted and acceptable philosophy of evaluation and it is not our intention to impose one. Instead we want to encourage you to consider and affirm your beliefs as you work through this book with us. Which of the preceding characteristics and axioms do you agree or disagree with? If you had to make a list of the strongly held beliefs that currently guide your approach to evaluation, what would it include?

## Considering Alternatives

If we believe that evaluation is done to improve education programs, then the design of evaluation procedures should be directly related to the program elements whose quality we are most concerned about or that we believe have the greatest potential to contribute to effectiveness. With this view, a standard evaluation design will not work for every program; evaluation planning becomes a unique and very specific procedure each time. Once again, this is evidence of our belief that practicing adult educators and their learners should hold ownership of the evaluation process. Problems typically surface when people feel that an evaluation plan they cannot support is being imposed.

To develop an effective evaluation plan, consider the major evaluation decisions that need to be made. Exhibit 2.1 introduces the commonly considered alternatives for each decision. Each of the decisions in the left column should be made while planning evaluation. Using those listed in the right column for each decision, evaluation planners can select one or any combination of alternatives that provides the information needed to determine the effectiveness of the education program (both process and results) in order to make improvements to it. The process will be repeated and different decisions may be made every time evaluation is planned for a new program.

The evaluation alternatives may remind you of the seven steps of planning you are asked to consider when making program decisions. As we strongly believe that the most effective evaluation planning occurs in conjunction with program planning, the relationship between the processes is intentional.

## An Example of Evaluation Planning

Work through an example with us to see how the five evaluation decisions are used to develop an evaluation plan for an educational program. An evaluation plan is being developed for an ongoing train-the-trainer program. The program has operated successfully for the past two years but some informal feedback indicates that organizations sending learners to the program are more satisfied with the results when the learners have some training experience instead of being new trainers. In this case, the following decisions are made for the evaluation plan. Remember that each decision is made after considering all of the alternatives listed in Exhibit 2.1.

## EXHIBIT 2.1. EVALUATION DECISIONS AND ALTERNATIVES.

| Evaluation Decision | Alternatives |
| --- | --- |
| 1. What is the *purpose* of the evaluation? | A. To aid in the design of the program<br>B. To provide feedback to learners and instructors during the program<br>C. To determine if learners developed important knowledge, skills, and attitudes as a result of the program<br>D. To determine if learners were able to use what they learned after completing the program<br>E. To determine if the program had the anticipated impact on people and organizations<br>F. Other purposes important to your program: |
| 2. *What* should be evaluated? | A. Changes in learners' knowledge, skills, and attitudes resulting from the program<br>B. Changes and improvements in the organizations for which the learners work<br>C. The design of the educational program, methods and procedures used, and instructor effectiveness<br>D. Other factors and results important to your program: |
| 3. What are the *sources* of evaluation information? | A. Learners' demonstrated knowledge, attitudes, and skills<br>B. Work completed by the learners<br>C. The instructor's perceptions and observations<br>D. Evaluation experts<br>E. Co-workers, supervisors, and others who interact with the learner<br>F. Other sources that are a part of your program: |
| 4. What are the *methods* for gathering information? | A. Formal or informal procedures<br>B. Direct or unobtrusive data collection<br>C. Designing specific evaluation tools or using existing learning activities for data collection<br>D. Attitude surveys, knowledge tests, or observations of performance<br>E. Oral, written, or demonstration activities<br>F. Other methods appropriate for your program and learners: |
| 5. *When* should evaluation be completed? | A. Before the program begins<br>B. Anytime during the program<br>C. Immediately at the end of the program<br>D. Some time after the program has ended when learners have had the opportunity to apply what they have learned<br>E. Other times that needed information is available: |

*1. What Is the Purpose of the Evaluation?* This first question is especially challenging because several of the alternatives seem to fit. As the program planners are
responsible for designing the train-the-trainer program, they could do evaluation
to aid in design improvements. They also might want evaluation to provide feedback during the program. However, it is important not to have too many purposes
for evaluation at one time or the design will be quite complex and the information
gathered difficult to interpret. So as the planners consider why they are planning
the evaluation they remember that concern was raised by the organizations sending learners to the train-the-trainer program: the program seems more successful
for experienced trainers than for inexperienced trainers. The purpose most directly
related to that seems to be: "to determine if all of the learners developed important knowledge, skills, and attitudes as a result of the program." If both new and
experienced trainers complete the program with the anticipated results, a second
purpose becomes important: "to determine if learners were able to use what they
learned after completing the program."

*2. What Should Be Evaluated?* Referring to the chart, the planners see that
they might evaluate changes in learners resulting from the program, changes in the
organizations for which the learners work, or the elements of the training program
itself. They decide that this evaluation will focus on changes in the learners because
there is interest in determining if the program has different results for experienced
and inexperienced trainers. The program design has been used successfully for two
years, so at this point there is little interest in evaluating the design and procedures
unless new information suggests it is not effective for the new trainers.

*3. What Are the Sources of Evaluation Information?* Several choices listed in
the chart are appropriate for this decision. The program planners decide to start
with the demonstrated knowledge and skills of the learners. They want to look
specifically at any differences between the two groups of learners—experienced
and new. They decide that if they do not find any important differences through
those methods they will seek input from the supervisors of the learners, who will
observe the learners' work after training is completed.

*4. What Are the Methods for Gathering Information?* Of the available choices,
it is decided to give specific knowledge and skill tests to all participants in the training program. Informal observations of learning activities had been used in the
past but had not identified the types of differences that seem to exist between
experienced and inexperienced trainers. Therefore more formal and specific evaluations will be used that focus on the knowledge and skills of the learners.

**5. *When Should the Evaluation Be Completed?*** The program planners want to be able to make improvements in the performance of new trainers if evaluations show they are not doing as well as more experienced trainers. Many opportunities to evaluate are available, ranging from before the program even begins until well after it is completed and the learners are back in their organizations conducting their own training programs. Again, however, the planners want the most direct and useful information to help them resolve the immediate problem. Therefore it is decided that evaluations will occur several times during the training program and a final comprehensive evaluation will be completed at the very end. If no important differences are found at that time, the evaluators will ask the supervisors to evaluate every experienced and inexperienced trainer after each has conducted a training program.

You can see that this evaluation plan provides the needed information to respond to the concern expressed about the program. If the program were being offered for the first time or if other questions were raised about its effectiveness a very different evaluation plan would be needed. This type of evaluation planning keeps the evaluation focused without using time and resources to gather information that is not considered important and therefore will not be used in the program. The example also shows how evaluation decisions are owned by the program planners, with input from the organizations with which they work. If it is learned that there are indeed differences in the results with new as opposed to experienced trainers, it is very likely that with this plan the evaluation results will contribute to improving the quality of the program. If no differences are found, the results can be shared with the organizations sending trainers to the program, which should help alleviate their concerns.

### *YOUR TURN*

We have found that applying the evaluation steps to a program with which you are familiar is an effective way to consider the potential of the process in giving you control of evaluation. We hope you will try it using the outline provided. Begin by selecting a program for which you are responsible. Using Exhibit 2.2 as an outline, work through the five evaluation questions and alternatives to determine the type of evaluation you believe would be appropriate for the program. After completing the outline answer the following questions.

- Who should you involve in developing the evaluation plan for the program?
- How would you and they make decisions?
- What would you add to these five steps to make the evaluation suitable for your program?

## EXHIBIT 2.2. YOUR TURN TO CONSIDER EVALUATION DECISIONS.

*Program selected for evaluation* _____

| Evaluation Decision | Alternatives |
|---|---|
| 1. What is the most important *purpose* of evaluation for this program at this time?<br><br><br><br><br>Why? | A. To aid in the design of the program<br>B. To provide feedback to learners and instructors during the program<br>C. To determine if learners developed important knowledge, skills, and attitudes as a result of the program<br>D. To determine if learners were able to use what they learned after completing the program<br>E. To determine if the program had the anticipated impact on people and organizations<br>F. Other purposes important to your program: |
| 2. *What* do you believe should be evaluated in the program?<br><br><br><br>Why? | A. Changes in learners' knowledge, skills, and attitudes resulting from the program<br>B. Changes and improvements in the organizations for which the learners work<br>C. The design of the educational program, methods and procedures used, and instructor effectiveness<br>D. Other factors and results important to your program: |
| 3. Of the *available sources* of evaluation information, which will you use?<br><br><br><br>Why? | A. Learners' demonstrated knowledge, attitudes, and skills<br>B. Work completed by the learners<br>C. The instructor's perceptions and observations<br>D. Evaluation experts<br>E. Coworkers, supervisors, and others who interact with the learner<br>F. Other sources that are a part of your program: |
| 4. What *methods* will you use to gather information?<br><br><br><br>Why? | A. Formal or informal procedures<br>B. Direct or unobtrusive data collection<br>C. Designing specific evaluation tools or using existing learning activities for data collection<br>D. Attitude surveys, knowledge tests, or observations of performance<br>E. Oral, written, or demonstration activities<br>F. Other methods appropriate for your program and learners: |

## EXHIBIT 2.2. YOUR TURN TO CONSIDER EVALUATION DECISIONS, cont'd.

*Program selected for evaluation* _____

| Evaluation Decision | Alternatives |
|---|---|
| 5. *When* is the most appropriate time to complete the evaluation?<br><br>Why? | A. Before the program begins<br>B. Anytime during the program<br>C. Immediately at the end of the program<br>D. Some time after the program has ended when learners have had the opportunity to apply what they have learned<br>E. Other times that needed information is available: |

# A Comprehensive System for Accountability

We have examined some basic principles of evaluation, but until now we have dealt with evaluation only as it would be done after an educational program has already been developed. If this procedure is followed three problems will likely result; as you read, see if they are familiar to you.

One problem is that evaluation may be ignored if it is planned separately from the program. Given the real time and resource pressures of delivering many educational programs, they often must be implemented quickly after (or even before) the planning is finished. Despite good intentions, the result is often that evaluation procedures are never developed or that evaluation is done on the spur of the moment, usually as the program is ending.

The second problem is that developing evaluation separately is usually more time-consuming and expensive. If an evaluation plan is actually completed it must be done by going back through the program plan to make all the evaluation decisions. Evaluation procedures and materials will have to be developed and added to the program; this certainly will take additional time to plan and execute and will require spending part of one's usually limited budget dollars.

The final problem with separating evaluation planning from program planning is that evaluations are often less objective if they are decided upon after the structure and delivery of the program have been determined. The natural hope and belief that the structure and delivery decisions were correct leaves the decision maker less willing to subject them to careful evaluation. Integrating evaluation into program planning will result in greater attention paid to it and a more efficient, inexpensive, and objective evaluation.

## The Accountability Process

This book is intended to help readers understand the principles of evaluation and to translate them into manageable procedures for evaluating education programs. One approach to evaluation, the *accountability process* developed by Paula Berardinelli and Jim Burrow, offers a systematic way to prepare a comprehensive, objective evaluation plan as an integral part of an educational program. This new approach to evaluation design was developed after an extensive review of research and theory supporting effective learning and evaluation procedures. The accountability process focuses on evaluation but clearly demonstrates the linkage between evaluation and program design. A systematic procedure to facilitate the application of the new evaluation procedure is explained in detail in Chapter Three; this section introduces you to the principles and major elements of the process. We describe how it incorporates the elements of effective evaluation while supporting your program planning efforts.

Figure 2.1 illustrates the theoretical framework on which the accountability process is based. Each element in the figure flows from the previous one as a result of systematic planning that considers the results expected from an education or training program. Each becomes a part of the evaluation process used to determine the effectiveness of the program and the relationships among its elements.

The accountability process begins with a clear identification of the purpose or results expected from the education program. Focusing on these will guide us to the learners' reasons for participating in the program and the changes and improvements in the learner that should result from it. In Chapter One we explained how the purposes and expected results of the Jubilee course were considered and incorporated as the needs assessment process was restructured. That maintained the focus on both the course and the learner's needs as redesign alternatives were being considered.

Educational planners should be aware of the skills, knowledge, and attitudes (SKAs) needed by the learners in order to achieve the purpose of the program. These SKAs may be identified as outcomes, objectives, content topics, or otherwise, depending on the program planning philosophy. The accountability process supports the educational planning philosophy that decisions about program design are made by analyzing the identified skills, knowledge, and attitudes. Instructional materials, activities, and resources are carefully selected based on which will most effectively and efficiently develop each of the identified SKAs consistent with the purpose of the program and with learner needs. In that way, evaluation can be used to determine not only if the specific SKA was developed but if the related instructional elements used to develop that SKA were effective.

Following the identification of the learning process, the model turns to anticipated results. Each important skill, knowledge, and attitude can and should be

## FIGURE 2.1. THEORETICAL FRAMEWORK
## OF THE ACCOUNTABILITY PROCESS.

Program *planning* identifies and anticipates
the relationships of these elements:

Purpose
of the
education
program

Learner
SKAs to be
developed

Education
program
design
decisions

Learning
that occurs
in the program

Changes
in job
performance

Organizational
improvement
resulting from
education program

Program *evaluation* measures the effectiveness
and relationships of these elements

measured while the learner is in the educational program. Change in SKAs resulting from the education experience is *learning*. The next step in the accountability process is to determine if the outcomes of the program are valuable and
used when learners return to their work and daily lives after completing the program. The effective use of skills, knowledge, and attitudes beyond the education
program is known as *transfer*; the accountability process encourages evaluation
planners to collect evidence of learners' use of the education program outcomes—that is, changes in skills, knowledge, and attitudes—when the learners return to their organization.

The ultimate goal, although a very difficult evaluation challenge, is to determine if the educational program had any effect on the organizations for which the
learners work. Those broad, long-term measures of organizational improvement
and effectiveness are known as *impact*. When fully implemented, the accountability

process assists those responsible for education programs to identify and track organizational impact measures for education and training efforts.

## Putting the Accountability Process to Work

Refer to the last three steps in Figure 2.1 to identify the program results that can be evaluated:

- *Learning*—changes in the learners' knowledge, skill, and attitudes that result from the program
- *Transfer*—learning from the program that is applied in the learner's work after completing the education or training program
- *Impact*—improvement in the performance of the learner's organization as a result of the learner's work

Each of the results is an independent measure; learning is distinct from transfer, transfer differs from impact. However, they are congruent. Without learning—a change in skills, knowledge, and attitudes—learners will not be able to improve their performance in the organization. In the same way, if learning is not transferred—taken back to the organization that employs the learner and used there—the organization will not benefit from the education or training program. Therefore a comprehensive evaluation process should allow for the measurement of all three types of results.

To help understand the evaluation process, visualize each of the three results of an education program as a dial, as shown in Figure 2.2. The needle on each dial will change based on the effectiveness of the education or training program. Our evaluation process gathers performance data that are represented by the position of the needles on each dial.

The dial on the left in Figure 2.2 represents learning. As the program develops the learners' skills, knowledge, and attitudes, the needle on the learning dial moves to the right. If the program is ineffective in changing the SKAs, the needle remains at the left. In the same way, the needle on the center dial, transfer, moves as learners are able to apply what they have learned when they return to their organizations after training. If learning does not transfer, the needle does not move. The dial on the right, impact, changes if the measures of organizational effectiveness improve as a result of the education or training experience. If the program has no effect on the organization, the needle remains stationary. When dials do not change or change only slightly, questions must be raised about the effectiveness of the educational experience.

Each of the dials is progressively more difficult than the one to its left; furthermore, each dial is dependent on the dial to its left. It is usually not difficult to

# FIGURE 2.2. THE DIALS TO BE MOVED: LEARNING, TRANSFER, AND IMPACT.

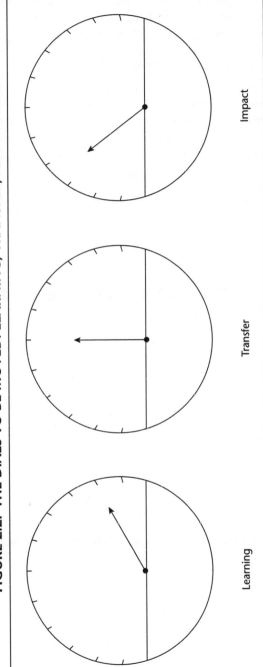

Learning

Transfer

Impact

identify some improvement in learners' skills, knowledge, or attitudes. However, it is more difficult to evaluate the performance of learners after they complete the program and return to their organization, and more difficult yet (but not impossible) to identify improvements in the organization directly resulting from an educational program.

It is the responsibility of adult education practitioners working with other stakeholders to determine what performance measures will be represented on each dial. True to the popular education principle of learner-centered teaching, the tick marks (measures) on the dials need to reflect the purpose of the education program and what the learner is expecting to accomplish. In other words, evaluation needs to be aligned with what is being taught—that is, with the achievement-based objectives. Alignment may be improved by keeping in mind that learning tasks are designed to facilitate learning, not to meet the needs of the planners or instructor. Figure 2.3 shows dials as they might be constructed for the Jubilee introductory course described in Chapter One.

## FIGURE 2.3. DIALS FOR THE JUBILEE COURSE.

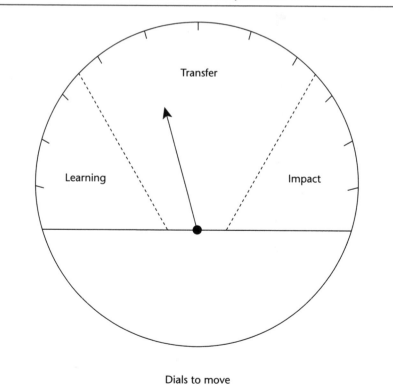

Learning

Transfer

Impact

Dials to move

### *YOUR TURN*

Figure 2.4 shows three blank dials representing learning, transfer, and impact. See if you can add descriptions for the tick marks on each dial for an educational program with which you are familiar. Make sure you start by identifying the purpose of the program and what the learners are expected to accomplish. Remember the differences between learning, transfer, and impact.

## Using the Accountability Process

We now show you how the accountability process works by applying it to Jubilee's Introduction to Popular Education course. We will use one achievement-based objective from the course to illustrate the progression of results for a participant in the course. The objective for the example is "participants will have practiced designing and using open-ended questions."

*Learning.* The first level of evaluation planning is learning. It determines whether participants have developed the skills, knowledge, and attitudes needed to achieve the objective. Learning is evaluated immediately during the educational program; the evaluation focuses on the specific SKAs developed in this part of the program. You can see from the following example that the measures listed include the necessary skill, knowledge, and attitude.

| | |
|---|---|
| RESULT | Learning |
| TIMING | Immediate and specific (within the course) |
| MEASURE | Can *differentiate* between open-ended and closed-ended questions |
| | Can *describe* the characteristics of an effective open-ended question |
| | Can *explain* why open-ended questions are an important practice |
| | Values the use of open-ended question by voluntarily *incorporating* them into lesson plans and discussions |
| | Writes and asks effective open-ended questions in designs and videotaped sessions |

### *YOUR TURN*

Use the program example you identified earlier when describing the dials. Select one objective and describe measures of learning that relate to the SKAs you believe should be developed in order to achieve the objective.

# FIGURE 2.4. DIALS FOR YOUR TURN.

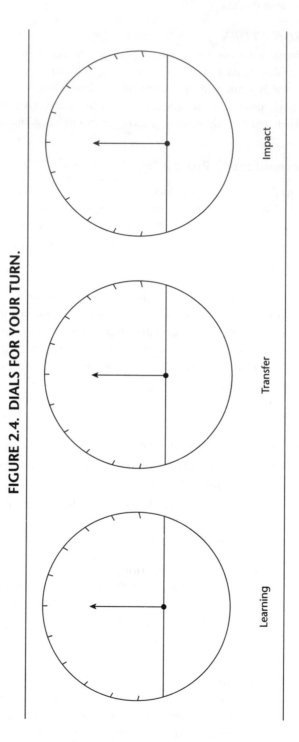

Learning

Transfer

Impact

| RESULT | Learning |
|---|---|
| TIMING | Immediate and specific |
| YOUR MEASURES | |

*Transfer.* The next level of results, transfer, is intermediate and applied. Evidence of transfer includes observable differences in the performance of learners after they have completed the education program and returned to their organization. What are they doing differently and better than before? The following example illustrates transfer measures for the Introduction to Popular Education objective.

| RESULT | Transfer |
|---|---|
| TIMING | Intermediate and applied (in the learner's work) |
| MEASURES | Incorporates open-ended questions regularly in all course plans |
| | Asks open-ended questions frequently in interactions with learners |

### YOUR TURN
Using the same program example and objective, identify the specific ways learners would apply the SKA to their work in the organization.

| RESULT | Transfer |
|---|---|
| TIMING | Intermediate and applied |
| YOUR MEASURES | |

*Impact.* Impact is the broad and long-term results of the education program: What difference did the program make to the organization as a result of learner performance? For many objectives it will be difficult if not impossible to identify impact measures. Often the program, even when provided to a large number of participants from an organization, will have only a modest effect on important organizational measures. Impact measures are usually identified through the mission statement of the organization, in an explanation of the reasons why the organization exists, or in agreed-upon organizational performance or productivity measures. In this example, the mission of Jubilee Popular Education Center is to celebrate autonomous learning:

| RESULT | Impact |
|---|---|
| TIMING | Long-term and broad (organizational) |
| MEASURES | Participants (in their roles as program planners) and teachers will come to view learners as subjects of their own learning |

and apply principles of popular education in an increasing number of courses and programs.

Course enrollments will increase in organizations that have sent participants to Jubilee courses as learners come to feel involved with and the subjects of their own learning.

### *YOUR TURN*

Using the program example you have been working with, take some time to define one or more impact measures you believe are related to the purpose of the program and the mission of the organization offering the program.

| RESULT | Impact |
|--------|--------|
| TIMING | Long-term and broad |
| YOUR MEASURES | |

## Examples of the Accountability Process

The accountability process has been developed to make evaluation objective, understandable, manageable, and useful. It allows practicing adult educators to focus on any or all of the three types of results—immediate and specific (learning), intermediate and applied (transfer), and long-term and broad (impact). Ideally, evaluation procedures are developed simultaneously with program planning decisions and the accountability process guides you through those decisions in order to match evaluation and program planning. Completing evaluation planning as a part of program planning is explained in Chapter Three through the use of a planning tool called the accountability planner. In Chapter Six we describe how we used the accountability process and the accountability planner to rethink and reformat the Introduction to Popular Education course.

We know that evaluation is often planned and completed after the educational program has been developed. The accountability process can be used that way; Chapter Four explains procedures to help you evaluate existing programs where evaluation was not planned at the beginning. Three case studies are presented in Chapter Five to demonstrate that type of use.

We believe the accountability process must be flexible. It follows important principles of evaluation and it requires objectivity, but it does not force evaluation planners into a system that is inconsistent with their program or their organization's resources. Evaluation is shaped around the program to help answer important questions: Did the program achieve its intended purposes? Was the program effectively designed and managed?

# We Stand on Their Shoulders

This book is not intended to be another evaluation reference; many good references exist that can help you understand evaluation philosophies and procedures. As we have said, this book is an extension of *Learning to Listen, Learning to Teach* (1994) and *Training Through Dialogue* (1995), both by Jane Vella, which have helped many people apply a popular education approach to the design and delivery of training and education programs. It resulted from recognition in the second book of the need to consider evaluation more thoroughly as a part of the planning process.

We three authors are students of evaluation and continue to learn. We are indebted to the many scholars and practitioners who have provided the groundwork for the accountability process and for this book. In this section we identify the scholars whose works most directly influenced our own.

## The Qualitative Tradition

Qualitative evaluation philosophies and principles guided Jane Vella's early work and still influence her evaluation decisions for Jubilee programs. Paula Berardinelli also advocates incorporating qualitative methods in the evaluation of educational programs. *Qualitative evaluation,* often called naturalistic evaluation, examines the qualities and characteristics of a setting or experience to develop understanding and determine meaning. Rather than isolating and manipulating elements for study, the qualitative evaluator is directly involved in a broader process of study and interpretation.

Qualitative evaluation is often used in an exploratory or formative way to gather information as a program is being developed. It allows study of a variety of program elements without clear definition of expected outcomes or clarification of criteria for evaluation. It also can be descriptive in that it can provide a richness of detail seldom available through quantitative evaluation.

Early proponents of qualitative models of research were Cronbach (1983) and Scriven (1967). Cronbach challenged evaluation systems that focus on objectives and outcomes exclusively and suggested that evaluation should be a concern of course developers in order to improve the course while development is still under way. Scriven extended Cronbach's argument to ask whether a focus on goal achievement is the only value of evaluation. He proposed that evaluators consider whether program goals are appropriate or worth achieving. Scriven recommended that evaluators use "goal-free" evaluation because, by discussing the program with participants, it might be possible to uncover unintended effects as well as ways to make the program more responsive to the learners.

Lincoln and Guba (1985) brought precision and structure to qualitative evaluations by proposing careful consideration of purpose, attention to related literature, purposeful selection of subjects, and the development of grounded theory through a process of induction. Excellent discussions of qualitative evaluation methods are offered by Babbie (1989), Lofland and Lofland (1984), Patton (1987), and Merriam (1988).

## Our Quantitative Roots

Burrow's work in the design and delivery of training programs for business and industry have made him an advocate and practitioner of quantitative evaluation. Berardinelli also uses quantitative methods in her work on transfer and impact evaluation. Quantitative studies are structured, precise, and focused on identifying and studying specific elements through measurement. Quantitative evaluations of educational programs focus on specific and direct measurement of outcomes. Evaluators using quantitative methods attempt to isolate and often manipulate important variables in order to document and ultimately predict performance and relationships.

Quantitative evaluation methods have been derived for curriculum models that emphasize goal and outcome identification. The father of goal-based evaluation is considered by many to be Ralph Tyler (1950), who established the clear connection between evaluation and education objectives. The planning process he proposed starts with a broad-based search for and selection of objectives. The objectives should be precisely and specifically stated in terms of expected learner behaviors and evaluation should be directed at determining whether those objectives are achieved. Program improvements are recommended when the curriculum is unsuccessful in accomplishing the objectives. In support of Tyler's model, Bloom (1956) and Mager (1972) designed methods for bringing greater precision and clarity to program objectives in order to focus on development and evaluation. Other excellent references for understanding quantitative evaluation methods are Popham (1988), Rossi and Freeman (1989), and Wholey, Hatry, and Newcomer (1994).

## Moving Toward Transfer and Impact

Leaders in encouraging education and training professionals to consider the transfer and impact of their programs are Kirkpatrick (1994) and Baldwin and Ford (1988). Kirkpatrick distinguished between four types of evaluation. *Reaction,* the most commonly used type, is a matter of asking participants what they like or dislike about the learning experience; *learning* involves informally or formally testing learners to determine the development of knowledge and skill during the program; *behavior* has to do with the change in job performance that results from the education or training program; *results* focuses on the effect of the program in achieving important organizational goals or measures.

A comprehensive analysis of theory and research related to training transfer was completed by Baldwin and Ford. It suggests that the factors most likely to influence performance resulting from training are training design, work environment, and the individual learner's characteristics. Baldwin and Ford identified specific elements within each of the three factors to be considered in program design and evaluation that appear to be linked to increased transfer of training. Berardinelli (1991) expanded on their analysis by designing and testing a model for predicting the impact of management training on organizations. The model can be used to identify program components for testing, predict relationships, generate hypotheses, and test those hypotheses in order to improve training effectiveness (Berardinelli, Burrow, and Dillon-Jones, 1995).

Berardinelli's theory of impact was developed in 1991 to test the complex relationships among educational program inputs and the results achieved. It relies on extensive review of research and theory supporting effective learning and the connection of evaluation procedures. The model focuses on evaluation as a means toward the goal of improved learning and organizational performance. Evaluation procedures and results are used to identify the elements of education programs through which people are able to apply (transfer) the knowledge and skills they learn to their work in order to have impact on organizational performance targets.

The structure of the evaluation process described in Berardinelli's work is based on a model of learning that has three variables. The model suggests that ultimate learner success—impact—is based on the interaction of the learning experience, the characteristics of individual learners, and the environment in which the learners apply what they learned after completing the educational program. Variables comprise elements that further define the way each variable affects the overall results of the educational program (see Figure 2.5).

The variables indicate that the learning experience can be improved through appropriate teacher activities and the optimum design of learning. In the same way, greater learning effectiveness results when the learner begins with the necessary levels of ability and skill, is motivated and expects to be effective, can commit adequate time to learning, and attempts to apply (transfer) what has been learned upon returning to the organization. The environment in which the learner works and tries to implement the new learning also may contribute to (or detract from) learning effectiveness. The primary elements in the work environment are

## FIGURE 2.5. VARIABLES AND ELEMENTS
## IN THE THEORY OF IMPACT.

Key: **Variables** (bold numbered items)
     *Elements* (italic items)

1. **Learning experience**
   *Teacher activities*
   *Learning design factors*

2. **Individual characteristics**
   *Ability and skill*
   *Motivation and expectation*
   *Time*
   *Transfer*

3. **Work environment**
   *Boss-colleague relations*
   *Reward system*

the relationship between learner and supervisor and the relationship between the rewards viewed as important by the learner and the resulting performance.

The accountability process presented in this book is a direct derivative of Berardinelli's theory of impact and the work of Baldwin and Ford. The process was developed as a part of Berardinelli and Burrow's consulting activities with organizations that were working to improve their education and training programs. However, unlike the theory of impact, the accountability process focuses only on the learning experience; the other two elements of the model are given only limited and incidental consideration. As you study the remaining chapters in the book and consider how the accountability process can be used in your programs, you may want to remember that additional improvements can be made by paying attention to the daily work environment of the learners and the personal characteristics and motivation of the learners.

### *YOUR TURN*

Now you have been introduced to the key principles and philosophy that guide the authors of this book in planning and conducting educational program evaluations. You have also reviewed the basic structure of the accountability approach to evaluation. Before you go further, revisit and reconsider in the light of what you have learned here the questions we posed at the beginning of the chapter.

- If you currently view evaluation as an important part of each program for which you are responsible, how does that show in the process as you evaluate?
- What key elements of a philosophy of evaluation that guide your efforts can you articulate?
- As a practicing adult educator, when do you feel that you have the autonomy to design evaluation in such a way that it helps you improve the education process as well as the results of the program?

You may already be thinking of evaluation differently from when you began reading the book. We hope you will continue to think about these questions as you consider our approach to evaluation in the remaining chapters.

CHAPTER THREE

# THE ACCOUNTABILITY PROCESS AND PLANNER

Through the ongoing testing and refinement of the theory of impact (Berardinelli, 1991) we observed the need for practitioners to have accessible evaluation tools. We believe the tools should also be accountable for learning. This chapter describes the accountability process and accountability planner we use to evaluate adult learning. Additional illustrations of the accountability planner are provided in Chapters Five and Six and in the Appendix.

Exhibit 3.1 shows the accountability planner. For ease of use and to show the relationships among the components of the accountability process, the planner is arranged in columns. Each column contains discussion of philosophy, definition of key terms, and procedural guidelines. As this chapter unfolds, we provide an exhibit highlighting each column in turn; every exhibit also includes an excerpt from the Jubilee course and from another training scenario, and you are given an opportunity to take a turn at completing an accountability planner for one of the programs in your organization.

Before beginning to complete the accountability planner, several initial decisions need to be made. These include two of the seven steps of planning, *who* and *why*: *Who* needs the education or training, and *why* do they need it? Also, using the five evaluation decisions and alternatives outlined in Chapter Two, the question "What is the purpose of conducting this evaluation?" needs to be answered. One final consideration is the first characteristic of effective evaluation discussed in Chapter Two, the need for evaluation to be objective. Having made all these decisions, let us proceed through each of the columns of the accountability planner.

EXHIBIT 3.1. THE ACCOUNTABILITY PLANNER.

| Column 1 | Column 2 | Column 3 | Column 4 | Column 5 | Column 6 |
|---|---|---|---|---|---|
| SKAs, Content, and Achievement-Based Objectives | Educational Process Elements: Learning Tasks and Materials | Anticipated Changes • Learning • Transfer • Impact | Evidence of Change • Content • Process • Qualitative • Quantitative | Documentation of Evidence | Analysis of Evidence |
| | | | | | |

## Column One:
## Skills, Knowledge, and Attitudes (SKAs):
## Content and Achievement-Based Objectives

The first column (see Exhibit 3.2) focuses on what the learner is expected to know, do, or believe as a result of the program. It includes the program goals and objectives and is defined by the content. Two additional steps of the seven steps of planning are operative here with specific responses to *what* (content) and *what for* (achievement-based objectives). The sources of the SKAs for this column can include any or all of the following: needs assessment, expert opinion, learner input, and organizational mandates. This content should also be specific and measurable as defined in the program planning process, and should be of value and importance to the organization. The content should be learner focused, action oriented, and related to applications the learner will make after the training.

*To complete column one:* List all the SKAs, major content topics, and achievement-based objectives for your program.

*Jubilee course example:* Knowledge = participants will have identified the generative themes of a group.

*Training example:* Objective = using a computer graphics or word processing program, the participant will have prepared a job aid that illustrates a specific job procedure in a way such that an employee can correctly perform the procedure each time the job aid is used.

### *YOUR TURN*

Identify an SKA, content area, or achievement-based objective from a program in your organization. You will use this example to complete a sample accountability planner within this chapter. Write your objective in the "your turn" section of column one in Exhibit 3.2.

## Column Two:
## Educational Process Elements

The second column (see Exhibit 3.3) focuses on educational process elements. It includes your responses to the three remaining of the seven steps of planning: *when, where* and *how.* Other process elements related to the Jubilee popular education program comprise the principles and practices and learning tasks. Other considerations of process elements, discussed in Chapter Four, include methods and activities, resources and materials, and instructors.

## EXHIBIT 3.2. ACCOUNTABILITY PLANNER: COLUMN ONE.

| Column 1 | Column 2 | Column 3 | Column 4 | Column 5 | Column 6 |
|---|---|---|---|---|---|
| SKAs, Content, and Achievement-Based Objectives | Educational Process Elements: Learning Tasks and Materials | Anticipated Changes • Learning • Transfer • Impact | Evidence of Change • Content • Process • Qualitative • Quantitative | Documentation of Evidence | Analysis of Evidence |
| Jubilee<br>Knowledge: Participants will have identified generative themes of a group. | | | | | |
| Training<br>Objective: Using a computer graphics or word processing program, the participant will have prepared a job aid that illustrates a specific job procedure in such a way that an employee can correctly perform the procedure each time the job aid is used. | | | | | |
| YOUR TURN | | | | | |

# EXHIBIT 3.3. ACCOUNTABILITY PLANNER: COLUMN TWO.

| Column 1 | Column 2 | Column 3 | Column 4 | Column 5 | Column 6 |
|---|---|---|---|---|---|
| SKAs, Content, and Achievement-Based Objectives | Educational Process Elements: Learning Tasks and Materials | Anticipated Changes <br> • Learning <br> • Transfer <br> • Impact | Evidence of Change <br> • Content <br> • Process <br> • Qualitative <br> • Quantitative | Documentation of Evidence | Analysis of Evidence |
| | Jubilee <br> Task 7, page 30, *Training Through Dialogue* <br> 1. Identify some of your own personal generative themes. <br> 2. Tell why you think it is imperative to know the generative themes of learners if you are using a popular education approach. | | | | |
| | Training <br> Examine samples of previously designed job aids, consult with experts and users (workers), and complete a software tutorial. | | | | |
| | YOUR TURN | | | | |

*To complete column two:* For each SKA, content area, or achievement-based objective listed in column one, identify the corresponding learning tasks in the training materials or development activities. Often there will be more than one process element for each SKA named in column one; it is not necessary to have one-to-one links between items in the first two columns.

*Jubilee course example:* Identify some of your personal generative themes; tell why you think it imperative to know the generative themes of learners if you are using a popular education approach. (See task seven on page 30 of *Training Through Dialogue.*)

*Training example:* Examine samples of previously designed job aids; consult with experts and users (workers); complete a software tutorial.

### YOUR TURN

Identify the corresponding process elements for the SKA, content, or objective you listed in column one.

## Column Three:
## Anticipated Changes (Learning, Transfer, and Impact)

In this column the changes (learning, transfer, and impact) anticipated as a result of the program are considered (see Exhibit 3.4). As indicated in Chapter Two, determinations of what should be evaluated need to be made at this point. This involves making a close match between organizational philosophy and elements that are important to the organization. A combination of content and process elements should be considered.

Anticipated changes are sequential. You need to look first at learning—the changes in SKAs that are immediate, specific, and focused on the individual before considering transfer and impact. Depending on the organization, there may be no need to consider transfer or impact. Transfer relates to changes on the job and are intermediate and applied; impact is long-term, broad, and focused on the organization. The latter is the most challenging to consider and is usually addressed with respect to the entire program rather than to specific SKAs.

*To complete column three:* Identify the specific anticipated changes that should result from the program. The changes will first be seen in the individual learner, then in the learner's job performance, and finally in organizational performance (impact). Start by selecting SKAs from column one that are most important or that you have an interest in measuring. For each, identify the specific change or changes you expect as a result of the program. Once you have identified the

## EXHIBIT 3.4. ACCOUNTABILITY PROFILE: COLUMN THREE.

| Column 1 | Column 2 | Column 3 | Column 4 | Column 5 | Column 6 |
|---|---|---|---|---|---|
| SKAs, Content, and Achievement-Based Objectives | Educational Process Elements: Learning Tasks and Materials | Anticipated Changes<br>• Learning<br>• Transfer<br>• Impact | Evidence of Change<br>• Content<br>• Process<br>• Qualitative<br>• Quantitative | Documentation of Evidence | Analysis of Evidence |
| | | Jubilee<br><br>Learning: Learners identify generative themes.<br><br>Transfer: Students show more energy for learning because their generative themes were included. | | | |
| | | Training<br><br>Learning: Increased knowledge of design principles.<br><br>Transfer: Increased use of job aids in training programs. | | | |
| | | **YOUR TURN** | | | |

changes for the learner, identify the specific changes that are most important for the learner's performance on the job (transfer). Finally, list any organizational changes you expect from the comprehensive and long-term implementation of the program (impact).

*Jubilee course example:* Learners identify generative themes (learning); students show more energy for learning because their generative themes were included (transfer).

*Training example:* Increased knowledge of design principles (learning); increased use of job aids in training programs (transfer).

### *YOUR TURN*

Identify your anticipated changes in learning, transfer, and impact.

## Column Four: Evidence of Change

This column contains the signs of evidence of change that you select (see Exhibit 3.5). They need to be direct, identifiable, specific, and accessible; they can include measures of both content-SKAs and process elements. Both qualitative and quantitative measures can be included. You need to be objective in identifying the evidence and able to clearly justify the relationship of it to the anticipated changes identified in column three. The relationship between columns three and four needs to be direct; however, you can have multiple measures of evidence for each anticipated change.

*To complete column four:* For each anticipated change identified in column three, name one or more specific measures that provide evidence of that change. It may be helpful to look for measures that already exist within the education program, on the job, or in the organization that relate to each specific anticipated change.

*Jubilee course example:* Generative themes of students are incorporated into lessons (learning); level of energy is high in the room during the program (transfer); students believe their themes are used and honored in the course (transfer).

*Training example:* Correctly identify the five design principles (learning); develop job aids using five principles of design (transfer); perform a task correctly with the job aid (transfer).

### *YOUR TURN*

Identify the evidence of change for each of the anticipated changes listed in column three.

**EXHIBIT 3.5. ACCOUNTABILITY PLANNER: COLUMN FOUR.**

| Column 1 | Column 2 | Column 3 | Column 4 | Column 5 | Column 6 |
|---|---|---|---|---|---|
| SKAs, Content, and Achievement-Based Objectives | Educational Process Elements: Learning Tasks and Materials | Anticipated Changes • Learning • Transfer • Impact | Evidence of Change • Content • Process • Qualitative • Quantitative | Documentation of Evidence | Analysis of Evidence |
| | | | Jubilee | | |
| | | | Learning: Generative themes of students are incorporated into lessons. Transfer: Higher level of energy in the room during program. Transfer: Students believe that their themes were used and honored in the course. | | |
| | | | Training | | |
| | | | Learning: Correctly identified the five design principles. Learning: Developed job aids using the five principles of design. Transfer: Task is performed correctly with job aid. | | |
| | | | YOUR TURN | | |

## Column Five:
## Documentation of Evidence

Decisions about documentation of evidence are recorded in column five; see Exhibit 3.6. These decisions are about the sources of evidence to use and when the evidence should be collected. It is most helpful to find sources of evidence that already exist within the program, are part of the job, or are identified within the organization. Developing a separate data collection instrument or using already developed instruments may by beneficial. Examples of already developed instruments are tests, work products, and activities. Several important needs should also be considered: specific documentation for each measure selected, development of a set of data collection procedures, and the validity and representative nature of the measures.

*To complete column five:* Identify a specific data collection procedure for each of the measures listed in column four. If necessary, prepare a data collection instrument and instructions for the collection of data.

*Jubilee course example:* Lists of themes are identified (learning); interview with participants is conducted to allow them to express their feelings about the use of their themes in the program (transfer); noise level in the classroom increases (transfer); participants are actively engaged (transfer); number of participants who are actively engaged in each learning task increases (transfer).

*Training example:* Pass a test with 100 percent accuracy on the principles of design (learning); create a correctly designed job aid (transfer); trainers use one or two job aids in each of the training sessions they design (transfer); improved job performance among people who have job aids (impact).

### YOUR TURN

Describe the documentation you will collect as evidence of the changes listed in column four.

## Column Six:
## Analysis of Evidence

After all the evidence is collected, gains or changes caused by the program need to be identified for the SKAs and content evaluated; this analysis appears in column six (see Exhibit 3.7). Other considerations include the time needed to collect and analyze data as well as the time you have allowed for the program. The number of measures included in the analysis, sample size, and types of analysis appropriate for the form of data you collect all shape your decisions on analysis.

# EXHIBIT 3.6. ACCOUNTABILITY PLANNER: COLUMN FIVE.

| Column 1 | Column 2 | Column 3 | Column 4 | Column 5 | Column 6 |
|---|---|---|---|---|---|
| SKAs, Content, and Achievement-Based Objectives | Educational Process Elements: Learning Tasks and Materials | Anticipated Changes • Learning • Transfer • Impact | Evidence of Change • Content • Process • Qualitative • Quantitative | Documentation of Evidence | Analysis of Evidence |
| | | | | Jubilee<br>Learning: Lists of themes identified.<br>Transfer: Interview with participants to express their feelings about the use of their themes in the program.<br>Transfer: Noise level in the classroom.<br>Transfer: Active engagement of participants.<br>Transfer: Number of participants who are actively engaged in each learning task. | |
| | | | | Training<br>Learning: Pass a test with 100 percent accuracy on the principles of design.<br>Transfer: Create a correctly designed job aid.<br>Transfer: Trainers use 1–2 job aids in each of the training sessions they design.<br>Impact: Improved job performance among people who have job aids. | |
| | | | | YOUR TURN | |

**EXHIBIT 3.7. ACCOUNTABILITY PLANNER: COLUMN SIX.**

| Column 1 | Column 2 | Column 3 | Column 4 | Column 5 | Column 6 |
|---|---|---|---|---|---|
| SKAs, Content, and Achievement-Based Objectives | Educational Process Elements: Learning Tasks and Materials | Anticipated Changes • Learning • Transfer • Impact | Evidence of Change • Content • Process • Qualitative • Quantitative | Documentation of Evidence | Analysis of Evidence |
| | | | | | Jubilee<br>Differences noted precourse and post-course and between participants who were asked and not asked about their generative themes. |
| | | | | | Training<br>Comparisons of job aids designed by trainers who took the design course and those who did not and contrast of pre-course job aids and postcourse job aids. |
| | | | | | YOUR TURN |

*To complete column six:* Determine how the data collected will be used in evaluating the program. Possible methods include trend analysis, comparative analysis of baseline information against ongoing performance, and comparative analysis of participants against nonparticipants.

*Jubilee course example:* Differences between participants before and after the course; differences between participants in this course who were asked about their generative themes and those in another course who were not.

*Training example:* Comparison of job aids designed by trainers who took the design course and those who did not; contrast between participants' precourse and postcourse job aids.

### *YOUR TURN*
Describe the ways you will analyze the evidence collected in column five.

Now that you have completed each column of the accountability planner in sequence, we hope you have a working understanding of this tool. Because we know that planning for evaluation does not always happen in such a sequence, in Chapter Four we discuss what happens when you need to "back in" to the evaluation of a program.

CHAPTER FOUR

---

# EVALUATING EXISTING PROGRAMS

---

E valuation poses some of the greatest challenges to people responsible for planning and implementing effective education and training programs. Though most educators want to know if programs are effective, circumstances often make it difficult to complete the types of evaluations where information is obtained that clearly communicates results achieved and program effectiveness. When educators are not comfortable with evaluation procedures or confident in evaluation results, it becomes relatively easy to make evaluation a low priority.

## The Reality of Ongoing Evaluation

Many evaluation experts preach that education evaluation should be developed as part of the program planning process or independently by objective outside evaluation experts near the conclusion of the program. But given the realities in many educational organizations, such requirements pose problems for those whose primary focus is providing education services to learners. Here are three common realities:

- Practicing adult educators tend to implement programs as they are designed. If evaluation has been ignored by program planners, there is little reason to expect that those who implement the programs will have the time, effort, and resources to develop and incorporate a comprehensive evaluation plan.

- Many predesigned programs do incorporate evaluation components, but the evaluation may not be comprehensive or even appropriate for a given use. Still, those responsible for implementing programs often trust the designers to make good decisions, so the specified evaluation activities are implemented as developed with the expectation that the results will be helpful in determining the program's effectiveness.

- Maybe the most difficult issue for educators to deal with is imposed external evaluation. Externally designed third-party evaluations can certainly be very effective and useful. However, they are often intimidating to those responsible for implementing the educational program, especially if the evaluators do not involve those responsible for implementing the program in planning the evaluation. The results may indeed be appropriate and useful to the organization requesting the evaluation (funding organizations, for example) but not particularly helpful and meaningful to those implementing the program or to the learners. In such instances, the people on whom the evaluation is imposed are not likely to be particularly enthusiastic or supportive of the evaluation activities.

We firmly believe that evaluation of education and training is so important that it should be a part of every program. Educators should be prepared and committed to completing effective evaluations within existing or new programs, programs that have good or inadequate evaluation designs, and programs for which they are totally responsible, as well as for those where they work with and respond to the needs of other organizations and agencies.

In the preceding chapters we introduced the accountability process and the accountability planner to provide a systematic way to consider evaluation from the beginning, integrated within the program planning procedure. Those chapters present the ideal and most effective evaluation planning procedure, but we recognize that such a procedure does not fit the reality of many practicing educators and trainers. The purpose of this chapter is to provide ideas on how to complete the same careful evaluation planning when faced with the more realistic circumstances just described. We refer to such situations as "backing in to evaluation." By that we mean taking the program as it exists and developing efficient and effective evaluation plans and procedures that meet the needs of those involved.

A term used in industry applies here: *retrofitting.* Products and processes are defined as retrofitted when they are redesigned and improved to meet a new need. By developing evaluation for an existing program we are in effect retrofitting it to meet our evaluation needs. We identify the program elements that can provide evaluation information as they are currently designed, modifying them when necessary to accomplish our new evaluation goals. We hope that whenever you plan a new educational program, you will consider integrating planning and evaluation by using the accountability process and the accountability planner. However, we also want to make evaluation accessible and practical within existing programs, so this chapter offers assistance in retrofitting them for the purpose.

Planning evaluation for an existing program has already been illustrated earlier in the book. In Chapter One we provided an example of how the needs assessment process was revised in the Jubilee Introduction to Popular Education course. The revision was decided upon in order to collect baseline data with which to compare future student performance. Though this was an important change in the program, it did not require a huge amount of additional time or resources to implement. With the new procedure, not only is evaluation of important course outcomes more precise but we believe the needs assessment itself is more effective. It improves both results and process. The information gathered provides a better understanding of the new learners and offers them personal insights that were not as clear previously.

After we explain the process for implementing the accountability process in existing programs, we devote an entire chapter to case studies illustrating the process. In Chapter Five, you will see how three organizations committed to the principles of popular education recently reviewed their programs using the accountability process to implement meaningful evaluation. In each of the cases, existing elements of the educational programs were identified that could be used to accumulate evaluation information. No changes were made in the program unless they were already planned as a part of ongoing program development and were supported by the program designers.

## Comparing Program and Evaluation Planning

We begin our study of how to plan evaluation for existing programs by looking at the common elements of program design and program evaluation. There are many similar elements in the two processes, so we should be able to use many parts of an existing education or training program to aid us in evaluation. Then we describe how to analyze an existing program in order to develop evaluation priorities. Once again you will see our commitment to ownership of the evaluation process by educators and learners and to autonomy in evaluation planning. We believe that those responsible for the program should make the evaluation decisions. This is especially true when adding evaluation, because the program has already been designed and its program planners have ownership of the design decisions. We end the chapter by providing examples of decisions and worksheets that can be used to organize the evaluation procedures for an existing program. You should be able to use the information in this chapter to develop evaluation procedures where none exist, to improve poorly designed evaluation, or to work with a funding agency or other organization in responding to its request for evaluation of an existing educational program.

### YOUR TURN

Consider the programs in your organization where evaluation is not done, is not as effective as you would like, or is imposed by others with different needs or expectations. What concerns do you have about these programs that you believe evaluation could help to resolve? What factors do you believe seem to interfere with completing the necessary evaluation?

Select one program and analyze it in the same way we did the Jubilee course in Chapter One. Using an existing procedure or learning activity from the program or by making a modest change, name one way you could collect evidence that would be helpful in determining the effectiveness of the program.

## Making the Connection

Evaluation works hand in hand with instruction. Instruction is planned to improve the knowledge and skills of learners; evaluation determines if the instruction is successful. Because of this direct relationship, instructional planning can often provide resources or results useful in evaluation. Exhibit 4.1 shows how by identifying the elements of effective instruction and considering the connection to evaluation.

Now we will analyze several of the elements to illustrate the use of the relationships in planning evaluation. Consider a goal for an adult education course on music appreciation: encourage participants to value a greater variety of music genres. With that focus the course planners will design activities to introduce learners to a variety of music types and help them understand and appreciate the differences. Using the goal for evaluation, the program will be successful if participants voluntarily select and listen to a greater variety of music categories after the course than they did before attending.

*Objectives* identify specific knowledge or skills that the learners will develop with standards identified to determine if learning is successful. For example, an objective may be: using a computer graphics or word processing program, participants will prepare a job aid that illustrates a specific job procedure in a way such that an employee can correctly perform the procedure each time the job aid is used. You can see how the objective provides a great deal of direction in planning the training program. The learner will need to develop skill in using a word processing or computer graphics program and will need to be knowledgeable

## EXHIBIT 4.1. COMPARING ELEMENTS OF
## INSTRUCTION AND EVALUATION.

| Element | Use in Instruction | Use in Evaluation |
|---|---|---|
| Goals | Identify the important results of the program | Identify the type of evidence to be used to determine program success |
| Objectives | Identify the specific knowledge and skills to be learned and the specific standards for success | Identify the knowledge and skills to be evaluated and specific standards to be met |
| Content | Provides the information learners must know in order to develop necessary knowledge and skills | Offers the basis for developing evaluation questions to test learner knowledge and skills |
| Methods/ activities | Provide structure for learning; the ways that learners interact with the content to develop knowledge and skills | Provide sources of evidence to determine learning; times and ways in which the learner is using what is being learned |
| Resources/ materials | Offer the sources of information or the means of delivering content and learning experiences for participants | Provide tools that learners are using during the program that can serve as sources of evaluation information or resources to assist in conducting evaluations |
| Instructor | Manages the learning process and supports learners and acts as a source of content in some programs | Manages the implementation of evaluation activities, serves as a source of evaluation information, and supports learners if they are concerned about evaluation |

about types of job aids and effective design principles. The learning activities must be specific and effective enough that the learners can develop effective job aids.

Now use the same objective to plan evaluation. You are able to identify what to evaluate (skill in developing effective job aids using a computer) and the level of effective performance that must be demonstrated when the learner is being evaluated (the employee using the job aid performs the job procedure correctly every time).

We will now review other elements of educational programs—content, methods, and activities—to demonstrate the relationship between program planning and evaluation. Instructional planners identify the content to be taught in the program to achieve the objectives. For example, a statistics instructor may choose to have students learn a number of formulas so that they can analyze data. Evaluation then would focus on those formulas to determine if students know each one. An interesting planning and evaluation decision in this situation would be if students needed to memorize the formulas or not.

Methods and activities are identified in a program to help students learn, practice, and apply the knowledge and skills. Instructional planners may choose to have learners role play an interaction between a customer and a salesperson to develop the learners' problem-solving skills. While the role play is occurring, the skills of the learner can be evaluated to determine if each has been developed.

## Selecting Elements to Evaluate

Whenever any of the planning elements occur in an education program there is an evaluation opportunity. Each objective, every activity, each instructional resource, and all instructor responsibilities can be evaluated. However, it is clearly not necessary or efficient to evaluate every time there is an opportunity. Especially in the pressure of planning evaluation for an ongoing program, evaluation priorities need to be established.

The selection process should begin by recognizing that evaluation focuses on two factors—the outcomes of the education program and the educational process. Outcomes or results are normally the most important factor to be evaluated; whether participants have learned and are able to use what they have learned is a critical evaluation question. However, educators also have a vital interest in determining the relative effectiveness of the various procedures and activities included in the program. Therefore, evaluation of the educational process is important as well.

Referring to the program elements listed in the previous section, the first two—goals and objectives—describe educational outcomes. The remaining elements—content, methods and activities, resources and materials, and the instructor—are a part of the educational process. It would be unusual when evaluating an educational program to exclusively focus on only outcomes or only the process. In most cases it is important to determine whether results have been achieved and if the procedures used were effective. However, based on unique circumstances or for a specific need, those planning evaluation may choose to concentrate evaluation efforts on one or the other of the two factors.

Consider a program established to train and certify nuclear power plant operators. The trainees' knowledge of job duties and ability to perform all duties accurately and safely is essential. In this situation, outcome evaluation may be the greatest priority. In another situation, a management development program that has traditionally been scheduled in a university classroom is now being transmitted to several sites simultaneously through a two-way audio-video television network. Because the delivery system is being changed, evaluators are most concerned about the effectiveness of the process at this time.

After the decision to focus on outcomes, process, or a combination, specific program elements should be reviewed and prioritized. Should goals, objectives, or both be evaluated? Which of the goals and objectives are most important? Are we satisfied with the content that has been selected for the program? Are we essentially satisfied with the content but concerned about one or two of the topics? Are the methods and activities well designed and implemented? Should others be considered? Are we making the most effective and efficient use of the resources and materials? Are there other resources that would be even more effective? Is the instructor well prepared, an expert in the subject matter, and an effective facilitator? This is just a beginning list of the variety of evaluation questions that can be asked. Because of limited time and resources, not all of the possible questions about program elements can be answered in the typical evaluation. However, none should be ignored in initial planning. From among all of the questions, evaluation planners should select those that when answered will provide information to judge the quality of the program and to make improvements if needed.

Because the intention of evaluation is to objectively determine the result and effectiveness of an educational program, we must be careful not to allow a great deal of personal bias and subjectivity to enter into the decision of what to evaluate. Those most intimately involved with a program will have the tendency to bring the greatest personal bias to evaluation planning. An effective way to reduce the bias and subjectivity in selecting evaluation elements is to follow a systematic decision-making procedure. An example procedure:

1. Review all program objectives and select those that describe the most important performance elements (knowledge and skills) needed by program participants.

2. Study the complete program design to identify the elements that are believed to be most critical to the effectiveness of the program.
3. Discuss the program with the developers and instructors to determine which design decisions they have questions or concerns about.
4. Identify the stakeholders in the educational program, including the learners, and determine their needs and priorities.
5. Determine the primary purpose for offering the program.

By completing all these steps, evaluation planners have a comprehensive list of the elements of the program that can be evaluated and factors that should be considered when selecting those to evaluate. At this point, the professional judgment of the planners will be used to select the final set of elements to be evaluated. The decisions should be reasoned and thoughtful but specific to the program. It would be difficult and normally inappropriate for people unfamiliar with the program to determine what elements should be evaluated. This gives ownership of the evaluation process to the people most closely associated with the program and who are responsible for the program's success. Examples of factors that might influence the selection of program elements to be identified are the following:

- Those considered most important to key stakeholders
- Those considered most important to the program's success
- New or untested elements
- Those that appear to be less effective
- Those for which data is readily available or easy to obtain
- Those that require limited additional time or resources to evaluate

## The Big Question: Should We Evaluate?

You might not expect that evaluators would suggest there are programs and times when it is inappropriate to evaluate. However, we must realistically recognize that there are circumstances when evaluation is not particularly helpful. If educators recognize the importance of evaluation and will objectively review results and apply findings, the process is valuable and an effective use of time and resources. If evaluation is not valued and there is little intention to carefully review and use results, there is no reason to design and implement even a simple evaluation plan.

A second reason to choose not to evaluate is when no clear purpose or objectives are evident for the program. It would seem that education programs should always have a clear purpose, but many do not. In that instance, if information is gathered about the program during evaluation, decision makers will have no guidance in determining whether the program has been successful.

Other reasons to question whether a program should be evaluated are these:

- If inadequate time and resources are available for the needed evaluation
- If stakeholders are satisfied with the design of the program and its results
- If the program is a one-time offering or a minor commitment of the organization

In summary, these are the essential requirements for effective educational evaluation:

CLEAR PURPOSE
COMMITMENT
RESOURCES
PERCEIVED VALUE

### *YOUR TURN*

Do you now see the connection between the elements of an effective education or training program and an effective evaluation plan? Review the written plan for one of your courses or programs and see if you can identify each of the elements that we have discussed. Then select two or three of those elements and develop a specific evaluation question for each. In your opinion, why would it be valuable to evaluate the elements you identified? What would the organization gain by having answers to the questions you developed?

## Steps in Evaluating an Existing Program

The accountability process for educational evaluation can be applied within existing program designs as well as in the development process for a new or revised program. Depending on the program elements that have been developed in the existing program, it may be possible to collect needed evaluation information without any additional design work. For a comprehensive evaluation process, some redesign or additional development of program elements may be needed. Implementing evaluation procedures into an existing program requires that the evaluation planners determine the evaluation information needed and then study the program to see if the information is available within the current design. In most cases, the only additional requirement will be to develop procedures for data collection and analysis.

## Evaluation Information Needed

In order to evaluate program effectiveness, two types of information are needed. The first category is learner change: Have learners increased their knowledge and understanding, improved their skills and performance, or changed their attitudes in line with the program's objectives? So, as we saw in Chapter Three, evaluation will attempt to identify changes in SKAs as evidence of program effectiveness (column one of the accountability planner). The second category is effective program design: Is the program designed and delivered to motivate learners and facilitate their learning? For this category, evaluation will attempt to identify effective characteristics of instructional activities, resources, and personnel (column two of the accountability planner).

So we see that the first step in planning evaluation within an existing program is to identify what can be evaluated. Evaluation planners need to review the current program plans and materials to identify (1) the critical skills, knowledge, and attitudes to be developed by the learners as a result of the program, and (2) the key activities, resources, and other program design elements considered to be essential to the success of the program.

## Methods of Gathering Evaluation Information

Often the first consideration when designing educational evaluation is formal testing of the learners. This is narrow, inadequate, and ignores major types of evaluation information needed as well as diverse methods of gathering information. Formal testing only measures learner performance and typically focuses on the knowledge of the learner; this alone will not provide adequate information to determine the effectiveness of instructional strategies and other elements of program design. In the next two sections we review a broader set of methods that can be used to gather evaluation information. These correspond to the documentation of evidence in column five of the accountability planner.

*Evaluating Learner Performance.* Many education and training programs include formal testing as a part of their design; the test results can be used to evaluate learner performance if the tests are well designed. When planning evaluation for existing programs, any tests used in the program should be reviewed to determine if they provide information that can document learner performance on critical knowledge and skills.

If formal tests are inappropriate, there are a number of other methods of measuring learners' skills, knowledge, and attitudes. Many of these are instructional activities built in to education programs. Examples of methods appropriate for evaluating learner performance include the following:

| Evaluating Knowledge | Oral questioning, discussions, writing assignments, class activities and assignments, work-related activities and assignments |
| | Formal testing including true-false, matching, listing, completion, multiple-choice, short answer, essay, case studies, problem solving |
| Evaluating Skills | Simulations of individual skills or complete tasks, games, projects, role plays |
| | Actual performance in the work environment of individual tasks or complete processes (actual or controlled working conditions) |
| | Observations of skills completed by the instructor, peer learners, experienced colleagues, supervisors, trained evaluators completed using checklists of tasks or performance elements, rating scales, descriptions of performance standards, written evaluations based on performance requirements, comparative rankings |
| Evaluating Attitudes | Self-perceptions |
| | The perceptions of others (customers, coworkers, peer learners, supervisors, instructors) |
| | Completed by direct observation, discreet observation, or recall of past experience using listings or descriptions of desired attitudes, descriptions of behaviors associated with the identified attitudes, Likert scales, forced choices, completion items, case studies, role plays |

Many ways to evaluate learner performance are already built in to education and training programs. When planning evaluation in an existing program, carefully review the program to determine where learners will be demonstrating key skills, knowledge, and attitudes. It is possible to collect information on learner performance at those times. Remember that evaluation can be either formal or informal and can occur at various times during a program. Also, through the use of simple and objective data collection procedures and materials, information can be collected in a variety of ways by a number of people involved in the program including the learners themselves. As we pointed out in Chapter Three, evaluation information is often included in materials completed during the program. These materials can simply be collected at the time of use and saved for later review.

*Evaluating Program Design Elements.* The critical result of most training programs is improved learner performance. Learner outcomes are also important in many education programs. However, the effectiveness of the instructional process is also an important outcome in both and deserves careful evaluation attention. For example, the Jubilee courses are designed according to the principles of popular education; Jubilee wants to determine if those principles are effectively incorporated and executed within the courses as well as in the programs planned by Jubilee Fellows. Most educators are concerned that their programs include elements such as well-written objectives, skillful instructors, appropriate instructional activities, and effective selection and use of materials and equipment.

Existing programs can be evaluated to determine the effectiveness of program design. Because the elements form the educational program, they can be evaluated by looking for evidence that documents the effectiveness of each. That evidence can be either the actual characteristics of the element or the results obtained as a result of the incorporation of the element in the program.

The initial step in evaluating program design is to identify the elements that are considered critical to the success of the program (column two of the accountability planner). Next is a more difficult step: describe the characteristics of each element to be evaluated that will be used to determine effectiveness (column three in the accountability planner). For example, an effective behavioral objective should include a clear and specific statement of the expected performance, a description of the conditions under which the learner will be expected to perform, and specific criteria that can be used to judge the learner's performance. Instructional materials used by learners should be easy to use, written at the reading level of the learner, objective, and clearly communicate needed information related to the learning objectives. To effectively evaluate an element in the program one must be able to identify the characteristics of that element based on principles of effective learning.

After identifying the characteristics of the element, name the anticipated and observable results of using the element (column four of the accountability planner). Expected results could be a direct relationship between specific objectives and program content, if well-written objectives have been included in a program. In the Jubilee course, these elements are named as *learning tasks and materials* (see Chapter Six).

Once characteristics and results are identified for each element to be evaluated, information-gathering procedures need to be developed (column five in the accountability planner). When evaluating the characteristics of an element, checklists can be prepared and each element can be reviewed using them. The checklists can be used by the program developers as a self-check, by learners as they participate in the program, by instructors, or by trained evaluators. Evaluation of many elements can occur before the program is implemented; others can be evaluated during the program.

For evaluating results, a similar procedure is used. The expected results are specifically identified and listed on a checklist or evaluation form. As the element is used in the program, observations are made or evidence is collected related to the expected results. Just as when evaluating learner performance, activities occurring within the program provide evidence to be used in evaluating program elements. In many cases materials can be collected and reviewed later to determine whether the element was implemented effectively or achieved the desired results. Evaluation planners should carefully review the existing program to identify materials and activities that provide evidence of the effectiveness of specific elements. Learners, education personnel, evaluators, or others can be involved at various times in making observations or collecting needed information for evaluation. After information has been collected a judgment can be made about the effectiveness of the element being evaluated using the expected characteristics or results identified previously (column six in the accountability planner).

## An Accountability Planner for Existing Programs

Careful planning and design of evaluation is necessary in order to complete an effective evaluation of an educational program. Because there are so many possible outcomes and elements to include in the evaluation, the use of a planning document will help organize it. You were introduced to the accountability planner in Chapter Three as an aid to planning evaluation as part of a new program. The discussion of evaluation planning in the previous section identified the appropriate accountability planner column corresponding to the evaluation decision being made. The accountability planner shown in Exhibit 4.2 has modified column descriptions to help you organize an evaluation plan for an existing program. In Chapter Five are examples of accountability planners and supporting materials developed for three case study organizations to help plan evaluation procedures for previously developed programs.

We must emphasize the limitations of fitting an evaluation plan to an existing program. If no modifications of learning activities and resources are made and the intent is to gather evaluation information through the existing design, some outcomes and process elements cannot be evaluated. Because data collection for evaluation may require additional time and effort on the part of participants and instructors, there may be a reluctance to incorporate evaluation into an already full program agenda.

A concern we often hear from program planners when we ask them to consider incorporating evaluation into existing programs is that it will interfere with

**EXHIBIT 4.2. DEVELOPING AN ACCOUNTABILITY PLANNER FOR AN EXISTING PROGRAM.**

| Column 1 | Column 2 | Column 3 | Column 4 | Column 5 | Column 6 |
|---|---|---|---|---|---|
| SKAs, Content, and Achievement-Based Objectives | Educational Process Elements: Learning Tasks and Materials | Anticipated Changes<br>• Learning<br>• Transfer<br>• Impact | Evidence of Change<br>• Content<br>• Process<br>• Qualitative<br>• Quantitative | Documentation of Evidence | Analysis of Evidence |
| Review all materials for the program and make a list of all important SKAs, content topics, and objectives that could be evaluated in order to determine if the learners have changed as a result of the program. | Review all materials for the program and make a list of all important learning activities, resources used, and instructor responsibilities that could be evaluated in order to determine the effectiveness of the program. | Select each of the elements from columns 1 and 2 that stakeholders want to evaluate. For each, identify the change or changes that are expected, indicating a specific outcome that has been achieved or a process element that was effective.<br><br>Consider changes that can be observed during the program (learning) or after the program (transfer) or a related organizational change (impact). | For each change in column 3, work with stakeholders and experts to identify the specific evidence that will be used to judge whether the change has occurred. Evidence can be both quantitative and qualitative. It can be immediate and specific (learning), intermediate and applied (transfer), or long-term and general (impact). The evidence identified should be available and accessible within the program or in the learner's organization. | For each item of evidence that is a learning outcome, review the learning program carefully to identify where, when, and how that evidence is demonstrated (group discussion, activity, role play, flip chart). For each transfer and impact element, look in the job setting to identify where, when, and how the learner will demonstrate the outcome.<br><br>Whenever a method of documentation is identified, match it to the related evidence from column 4. | For each anticipated change identified in column 3, describe how the evidence collected will be analyzed to determine if the educational program was effective in achieving that change. An analysis method should be identified for each type of evidence being collected.<br><br>Consider comparison of precourse and postcourse performance, comparison of participant and nonparticipant performance, comparison to an established standard, and so on. |
| | | | | | |

the learning process or detract from the collaborative atmosphere that has been developed. This concern often stems from the traditional view of evaluation as negative and judgmental rather than as an effective means of providing feedback and improving the learning process. In this situation, we need to respect the program planners. Evaluation in these circumstances should be limited to existing evidence that is part of the program until planners and learners become more comfortable with the broader view of evaluation. Only a limited amount of evaluation information will be available and it may be decided that the resulting data cannot provide adequate information to warrant evaluation attention.

### *YOUR TURN*

What differences do you see between developing evaluation as part of program planning and adding an evaluation plan to an existing program? In considering the procedures to decide which should be used in your organization, what would be the advantages and disadvantages of each? Which would you recommend? Review an existing education or training program. Using the blank rows in the accountability planner in Exhibit 4.2, see if you can complete all six columns with information from the program for one SKA, content topic, or objective. Remember, if evaluation is not an important focus in program planning, there may not be adequate information in the program materials to complete every column.

## CHAPTER FIVE

# THREE EXAMPLES

Thousands of educators representing hundreds of organizations have participated in the Jubilee courses or read the two Jossey-Bass books cited earlier to learn about popular education and to integrate its principles and practices into their adult education programs. A frequent question is: How do we know it works? This book describes a process that helps answer that question. To begin the process of determining the effectiveness of Jubilee courses, we identified three organizations that have sent program planners to Jubilee for training. They all integrate popular education into their programs in different ways; each agreed to participate in the development of an evaluation plan for one of their programs using the accountability process and the accountability planner. This chapter describes the planning process for each organization using this model. It illustrates how the process can work in varied organizations and program designs.

The case studies are presented by examining each organization and the nature of the education or training program for which evaluation was planned. Then an example from the accountability planner for the program is presented. Each case concludes with an analysis of the process and comments of program planners from the organization on their perceptions of the process.

Each of the cases was developed using a "backing-in" process because the programs had already been designed. We recommended that they use the accountability planner based on a review of program materials, but each organization made the decisions about what should be included in its final evaluation plan.

## Completing the Accountability Process

We collaborated with the program planners from each organization by explaining the accountability process and designing the accountability planner for the selected program. Recognizing the importance of the learners as subjects and their autonomy in decision making, each organization decided what information it wanted to incorporate into the data collection process. After each accountability planner was complete and the needed data collection instruments were prepared, they were sent to the organizations for use in their program.

You will realize when you review the examples from the accountability planner that information for some columns is not available. Programs that are planned without consideration of the evaluation questions that arise in the planner will often not include all of the named planning decisions. Rather than modifying the program, the evaluation process for the case studies continued, using available information. After completing the evaluation and being given an opportunity to revise the program, planners could choose to incorporate the missing information or not.

Remember that these case studies are provided to illustrate this evaluation of the popular education approach of Jubilee. These accountability planners were designed to determine the effectiveness of popular education principles and practices, not of the specific program offered by the organization.

## Case One: NETWORK's Voter Education Program

NETWORK is a national Catholic social justice lobby founded in 1971 by forty-seven religious women. It is a nonprofit, membership organization of lay and religious women and men who put their faith into action by lobbying to influence public policy in Washington, D.C. NETWORK's political lobbying goals are to secure just access to economic resources, reorder federal budget priorities, and transform global relationships.

For the past twenty-five years, NETWORK has educated and lobbied for social change. Its purpose is to create a society that respects the dignity of each individual, promotes the good of all, provides just access to the nation's resources, and is attentive to the needs of people who are poor.

NETWORK professes that participation of all citizens in the formation of public policy is one key building block leading to a just society. NETWORK therefore complements lobbying on Capitol Hill with education of U.S. citizens on the issues before federal legislators, on how government functions, and on participation in the democratic process.

The board of directors of NETWORK urged the staff to make voter registration education a priority. Kathy Thornton, Mary Ann Smith, and Michael Culliton of the NETWORK staff came to North Carolina in August 1995 to study the Jubilee approach to popular education and to prepare the first draft of a voter registration education program that would be in place for the 1996 national elections. The three had long experience in adult and community education. They needed to define a single popular education approach that would be appropriate to the wide and diverse national audience they hoped to reach.

## The Education Program

The program developed was print-based, structured around a facilitator guide and the materials and resources needed to offer the voter education program. Seven community-based groups conducted training programs to pilot test the draft materials. Feedback from the planners and organizers of those programs was critical in shaping the final set of training materials that was used to prepare the accountability planner. The accountability process was developed to evaluate the effective integration of popular education concepts and procedures into the voter education program.

*Our Voices, Our Vote* is a printed program guide providing detailed instruction and resources to be used by facilitators as they conduct a voter education program. It relies exclusively on volunteer organizations and individuals to use the materials as designed to offer the program. Because the program was designed using the principles and practices of popular education, it provides an excellent case for applying the accountability process and accountability planner to an existing program.

The program guide provides an introduction to facilitators on the principles of popular education. It also includes guidance on preparatory activities to be completed prior to the program. The voter education program is developed through fifteen learning tasks ranging from learning task one, life experience symbols, to learning task fifteen, celebrating. The program was especially designed for people who are not registered to vote or who, though registered, need education regarding the importance and power of their vote. The achievement-based objectives were that the participants, by the end of the program, will have done the following:

- Reviewed a brief history of voting in the United States
- Identified reasons to vote
- Reviewed the symbols of and three descriptive statements about the major political parties
- Actually registered to vote if they had not yet done so
- Practiced using a voting machine or completed a simple ballot

## The NETWORK Accountability Planner

Exhibit 5.1 shows a section of the accountability planner prepared for the *Our Voices, Our Vote* program. As with each case in this chapter, we select an important section of the program rather than the entire accountability planner to demonstrate how the accountability process was applied in an existing program. In this example, the evaluation is directed at determining if a comprehensive printed facilitator's guide without face-to-face train-the-trainer support can effectively integrate the principles and practices of popular education in programs delivered through volunteer organizations.

The completed accountability planner describes the evaluation plan to assess the effectiveness of *Our Voices, Our Vote* in integrating principles and practices of popular education through its materials. Because of the voluntary nature of the program and the difficulty of following up with participants after completion of the program, the accountability planner was developed to evaluate learning only, not transfer or impact. In the next section we describe how transfer and impact measures could be developed for the program.

Exhibit 5.1 actually shows the third revision of the planning document. The authors worked with NETWORK personnel to develop the final plan by reviewing the program materials, suggesting evaluation ideas, and listening to their feedback. It was important for the evaluation plan to meet the needs and expectations of the organization, so decisions to include or exclude items were made by NETWORK.

As the accountability planner is a planning document, its format is usually not efficient for actually recording data for analysis. Once agreement was reached on the planner, outcome documentation forms were prepared that made it easier to collect and record information. Those forms were provided to volunteer facilitators with instructions for their use. One of the forms used to collect evidence for the learning tasks identified in the accountability planner is shown in Exhibit 5.2. Notice that two additional columns were added in order to identify learners who were engaged in the learning task but may not have completed the final product. This requires a bit more time for the facilitator or observer to record the information, but it could be meaningful data for program planners.

The form shown in Exhibit 5.3 was requested by NETWORK personnel. We discussed the value of qualitative data as a part of the evaluation process in Chapters One and Two. Qualitative feedback has been an important part of Jubilee courses; NETWORK personnel chose to collect qualitative information using the questions on the form, which is to be completed by the facilitator. The responses to these questions are in a real way evaluation indicators of transfer, as the facilitators respond with their perceptions of popular education developed as a result of their use of the materials on the job.

# EXHIBIT 5.1. ACCOUNTABILITY PLANNER: OUR VOICES, OUR VOTE.

| Column 1 | Column 2 | Column 3 | Column 4 | Column 5 | Column 6 |
|---|---|---|---|---|---|
| SKAs | Educational Process Elements: Learning Tasks and Materials | Anticipated Changes | Evidence of Change | Documentation of Evidence | Analysis of Evidence |
| Learning task 1: life experience symbols | Select a life experience Draw a simple picture Share your story | Learner engagement | Number of learners who create symbols of their life experience | Facilitator or assistant observes learners while they work | Compare number of learners who create symbols to number who did not |
| Learning task 2: naming our strengths | Select and share a word Prepare a SNOW card Share your work | Learner engagement | Number of learners who created SNOW card | Photograph of SNOW card display or recording of numbers of SNOW cards | Compare number of learners who prepared card to number who did not |
| Learning task 4: session feedback | Share likes and suggestions in pairs | Feedback | Number of things liked and suggested changes | Notes of assigned note takers Listening by facilitator during sharing Items recorded on feedback chart | Compare items listed in early and later feedback sessions to determine response to learner feedback |
| Learning task 5: dreaming a new world | Identify a change you would make in the world Share your dream | Congruence and integration | Number of changes that connect dreams and preparation to vote | Facilitator or assistant listens to ideas | Number of ideas that connect dreams and preparation to vote compared to number that do not connect |
| Learning task 7: a bumper sticker | Create a bumper sticker Share it with the group | Synthesizing learning | Number of learners who created bumper stickers | Photograph of bumper stickers on chart | Compare number of learners who created a bumper sticker to number who did not |

| Learning task | Activities | Category | Number measure | Observation | Comparison |
| --- | --- | --- | --- | --- | --- |
| Learning task 9: registering to vote | Listen to procedures<br>Fill out registration card<br>Share feelings | Took action | Number of nonregistered voters who registered | Facilitator or assistant observation | Compare number of nonregistered voters who registered to number who did not register |
| Learning task 10: session feedback | Share likes and suggestions in pairs<br>List questions on the chart | Feedback | Number of things liked and suggested changes<br>Number of questions added to the chart | Notes of assigned note takers<br>Listening by facilitator during sharing<br>Items recorded on feedback chart | Compare items listed in early and later feedback sessions to determine response to learner feedback |
| Learning task 11: slogan time | Create a slogan sign | Focus on content | Number of slogans created | Collect signs or use facilitator or assistant observation | Compare number who completed slogan signs to number who did not |
| Learning task 13: session feedback | Share likes and suggestions in pairs | Feedback | Number of things liked and suggested changes | Notes of assigned note takers<br>Listening by facilitator during sharing<br>Items recorded on feedback chart | Compare items listed in early and later feedback sessions to determine response to learner feedback |
| Learning task 15: celebrating | Receive certificate<br>Recognize voter registration<br>Share refreshments and company of the group | Accomplishment | Number of learners who completed the voter registration program | Number of certificates given | Compare number of participants who completed all sessions to number who began session |

## EXHIBIT 5.2.  FACILITATOR GUIDE'S
## PROGRAM OUTCOME DOCUMENTATION.

| Learning Task | Number Actively Engaged in Activity | Number Who Shared Information | Outcomes Created from Learning Task (list how many of the following items participants developed) |
|---|---|---|---|
| 1. Life experience symbols | | | _____ created symbols |
| 2. Naming our strengths | | | _____ created SNOWs |
| 3a. Gallery walk | | | |
| 3b. Gallery walk questions | | | |
| 4a. Session feedback | | | _____ things liked<br>_____ changes suggested |
| 4b. Questions chart | | | _____ questions added to the chart |
| 5. Dreaming a new world | | | _____ connections identified |
| 6. Who votes today | | | |
| 7. A bumper sticker | | | _____ created stickers |
| 8. Donkeys and elephants | | | |
| 9a. Registering to vote | | | _____ registered to vote |
| 9b. Words for registering | | | |
| 10a. Session feedback | | | _____ things liked<br>_____ changes suggested |
| 10b. Questions chart | | | _____ questions on chart |
| 11. Slogan time | | | _____ completed slogans |
| 12. Completing a ballot | | | |
| 13. Session feedback | | | _____ completed feedback forms |
| 14. Register or vote commercials | | | |
| 15. Celebrating | | | No. beginning _____<br>No. completing _____<br>No. in 1st session _____<br>No. in all sessions _____ |

## EXHIBIT 5.3. QUALITATIVE QUESTIONS FOR NETWORK.

**Instructions:** The following questions are designed to gather your opinions on several popular education components of the NETWORK program Voter Education: Our Voices, Our Votes. After you finish the program please record your information in the space provided (attach additional sheets, if necessary).

1. As a facilitator, what is your previous experience in using a popular education approach?

2. What surprised or delighted you about using a popular education approach to facilitate this program?

3. What obstacles or problems did you, as a facilitator, encounter in using a popular education approach?

4. In what ways was your preparation for facilitating Voter Education: Our Voices, Our Vote different from the way you have prepared to facilitate other programs? In what ways was your preparation similar?

5. Aside from achieving the program objectives, please share any other results, outcomes, or effects of this program for yourself and for the participants.

---

## Using the Evaluation Results

Most people who complete an accountability planner for their program and collect the evaluation information realize that they have an extraordinary amount of data. If the learning activities built in to the program design are used to gather information, as NETWORK did, only a limited amount of time and effort will be required for evaluation activities during the time the program is being conducted. The procedures used to organize, analyze, and interpret the evaluation information need to incorporate the characteristics discussed in Chapter Two: effective evaluation is objective, identifies important program elements, matches the organization philosophy, uses measures that are identifiable and accessible, and focuses on both outcomes and process.

An initial review of the data collected identifies which achievement-based objectives that have measures available were accomplished successfully. Because the analysis of data typically compares the number of learners who successfully completed the task to the number who did not, ineffective outcomes should be readily apparent, as should those that were most effective. Because each measure is directly matched to a list of educational process elements, the most effective elements in developing a given SKA and those that were less effective can be identified. When an outcome is not achieved at a level considered appropriate by the organization, that section of the program materials can be carefully reviewed to determine how it can be strengthened. NETWORK personnel review the qualitative responses as well to determine if there are insights into strengths and weaknesses of the program. The collected data provide an objective basis for NETWORK to judge whether the program as implemented through the volunteer organizations was effective in utilizing the principles and practices of popular education as demonstrated by the SKAs of the participants (outcomes) and the results of the learning activities used (process).

An important benefit of this evaluation case study is derived by Jubilee. The data from the accountability process is evidence of the transfer and impact of the Jubilee courses. The NETWORK personnel involved in the design of the *Our Voices, Our Vote* program had participated in the Jubilee introductory course; one person had completed the advanced course. By reviewing the NETWORK program materials (using an additional accountability planner not included in this chapter) and the data collected by NETWORK, Jubilee can determine if the Jubilee Fellows demonstrate the SKAs developed through the course when they return to their organizations. Their efforts in the program design are evidence of transfer.

Even more exciting is the impact Jubilee will be able to document as they review the evaluation results returned by the volunteer organizations who use the NETWORK materials. Recall that Jubilee's mission is to celebrate autonomous learning. As many organizations effectively integrate the principles and practices of popular education using NETWORK programs and as the evaluation results provide evidence of autonomous learning, the achievement of that important outcome will be evident.

## Possible Next Steps

The evaluation process developed and implemented by NETWORK is clearly sufficient for effective evaluation. It meets the characteristics and qualities of effective evaluation and responds to the organization's concerns. It provides evidence of the achievement of outcomes and the effectiveness of the educational program.

The accountability planner developed for the existing program identified parts of the program where there are no directly related components—SKAs, learning activities, or the like; also, sometimes the program activities did not generate identifiable and accessible measures of learner performance. Both are common findings when first efforts are made to match evaluation planning with program design. As NETWORK reviews and revises the program or develops similar programs in the future, missing elements can be developed, needed relationships among program elements strengthened, and more accessible measures implemented.

We encourage all organizations responsible for education programs to consider how to measure transfer. NETWORK is an excellent case of transfer measures being directly related to the program's purpose. The *Our Voices, Our Vote* program is directed at voter education with the intent to increase personal perception of power in voting and responsibility to cast a vote. Without a measure of learner actions when they complete the program and return to their daily responsibilities, the full effectiveness of the program cannot be determined. What transfer measures would be appropriate for this program? The apparent outcome is that people who were not previously registered to vote did indeed vote in the next election after participating in the program. The connection between that action and participation in the program is not absolute. Certainly other factors could interfere with the best intentions of the individual to vote. However, a follow-up look at voting records to determine the percentage of program participants who voted compared to a similar group of people who did not participate in the voter education will offer evidence of transfer. In addition, follow-up surveys or discussions with participants can elicit information on their continued perception of the power of their vote.

In the long run, important impact measures for NETWORK related to this program are increasing voter registration and voting rates in the communities where the programs are held, greater participation of citizens in the political process, and other related factors. Continuing use of the accountability process and the accountability planner as a part of program planning should help NETWORK to identify and measure important learning, transfer, and impact results for its programs.

## Case Two: University of Washington's Extended MPH Program

The program objectives of the extended Masters in Public Health (MPH) degree program at the University of Washington are to provide graduate education opportunities for employed mid-career professionals practicing in the fields of public, community, school, or environmental health. Graduate students do not interrupt their employment but rather come to the university for four weeks of intensive residence study for three consecutive summers and complete two academic years of course work through directed independent study. They attend four on-campus weekend seminars at two-month intervals during the first two academic years and complete a thesis or work-related project.

In 1994, Robert Collins, director of the Health Education Pathway in the extended MPH degree program read *Learning to Listen, Learning to Teach*. He called Jane Vella to tell her he was using the book as a text for a course entitled Application of Learning Theory to Health Education and asked her to come to Seattle to meet the graduate students on their last weekend session. During the visit, they talked of Collins's hope of revising the course curriculum to teach the principles and practices of popular education as they apply to health issues. The most recent revision of that graduate curriculum was used as the basis for this case study.

## The Education Program

HSERVE 525, otherwise known as Application of Learning Theory to Health Education, is a course required of all graduate students enrolled in the Health Education Pathway of the extended MPH degree program. The purpose of the course is to help students who are practicing health educators to apply popular education theory and practice in the preparation, presentation, and evaluation of health education. The course is offered through five on-campus meetings spread throughout the first academic year, totaling twenty-six contact hours and additional off-campus work developing and applying course concepts and meeting with instructors.

Course content is developed around three topics:

- *Learning theory:* background from andragogy and self-directed learning along with popular education, including Vella's twelve principles of learning
- *Learning styles:* exploration of a variety of learning styles, their common elements, and their implications for teaching and learning, self-assessment, and assessing needs and capacities of various populations
- *Presentation skills:* Exploration of a variety of issues and practice approaches to developing more interesting and effective health education learning experiences, including anticipating needs of target audiences, dealing with the social dynamics within a group, and experiential learning strategies

The course planners developed learning modules for each session following the popular education model and the seven steps of planning. Each module included an agenda structured around achievement-based objectives with a set of learning tasks and a student learning guide describing the learning procedures for each task. While planners were working with Jubilee in the preparation of this case study, they were planning the 1996 course. Course materials were being revised based on Teresa Buckland's participation in the Jubilee course. The accountability planner prepared by Paula Berardinelli and Jim Burrow was based on the materials for session one of that 1996 course. The achievement-based objectives were for each student to have done all the following by the end of session one:

- Used a warm-up
- Reviewed how groups work with optimal participation
- Distinguished between monologue and dialogue
- Identified generative themes of a group
- Practiced designing and using open questions
- Used and evaluated selected principles and practices of popular education

After session one had been completed and using the session's accountability planner as a model, the course developers planned to create an accountability planner for session two as a part of the course revision process.

## University of Washington Accountability Planner Example

The accountability planner for session one, shown in Exhibit 5.4, is based on twelve learning tasks; they are listed in column one. Column two describes the learning activities students are asked to complete for each task. Column three is blank because anticipated changes were not specifically identified in the materials. Column four lists the evidence that could be tracked to measure achievement of each SKA. The evidence was developed from the activities students were asked to complete for the learning task. Column five identifies the data to be collected from the activities in order to document the evidence. The analysis of that data was the responsibility of the two instructors, who reviewed, examined, and critiqued work-related designs prior to each session.

## Using the Evaluation Results

The accountability planner shown in Exhibit 5.4 is the first draft prepared and presented to the planning team for the University of Washington course. It was not used as a part of session one because too little time was available between completing revision of the materials and the scheduled session date.

In addition, course planners had several concerns about the accountability planner process that needed to be resolved before they felt comfortable using it to collect evaluation information. The primary concern was that the program

# EXHIBIT 5.4. ACCOUNTABILITY PLANNER FOR HSERVE 525: SESSION ONE.

Instructions: This form is designed to gather information on the effectiveness of each session of the course in developing the identified skills, knowledge, and attitudes (SKAs). Please carefully collect the information requested and record it on the form. Information needed is matched to the learning task in which the specific SKA is to be developed. *Try to complete each item as soon as possible after the requested information is available.* It may be helpful to identify an assistant or other volunteer to be responsible for gathering and recording the requested information. Some of the information can be collected and recorded during the program when the specific learning task is completed. Other information cannot be recorded until late in the session when later activities are completed.

| SKAs, Content, and Achievement-Based Objectives | Educational Process Elements: Learning Tasks and Materials | Anticipated Changes | Evidence of Change | Documentation of Evidence | Analysis of Evidence |
|---|---|---|---|---|---|
| Knowledge, Skills— how to use a warm-up | Task 1 | | Participation in warm-up activity Partner sharing Large-group discussion Written reflection | _____ Completed all warm-up activities  _____ Shared both the symbol and personal information with partner  _____ Actively engaged in large-group discussion  _____ Completed reflection statement demonstrating understanding of effective warm-ups | |
| Knowledge— safety as a group participative method | Task 2, white handout | | Written reflection Small-group agenda review Personal expectation identification Writing SNOW cards Reading and questioning | _____ Completed reflection statement demonstrating understanding of safety  _____ Participated in agenda review and personal expectation identification  _____ Developed SNOW cards  _____ Read handout and affirmed understanding | |

| Knowledge/Objective | Task | Activities | Assessment |
|---|---|---|---|
| Knowledge—accountability as a group participative method | Task 3, chart: how adults learn | Identifying important sections of reading<br>Describing and analyzing learning situations<br>Writing SNOW cards<br>Understanding adult learning research | ___ Circled relevant section of the reading<br>___ Participated in paired sharing activity<br>___ Developed SNOW cards<br>___ Affirmed understanding of adult learning research |
| Knowledge—respect as a group participative method | Task 4 | Identifying important sections of reading<br>Small-group discussion | ___ Circled relevant section of the reading<br>___ Participated in small-group discussion |
| Knowledge—the learners are decision makers concept as a group participative method | Task 5, lecture | Listening to a lecture<br>Small-group discussion<br>Recalling examples | ___ Identified personal example in small groups<br>___ Identified example that demonstrated understanding of the method |
| Knowledge—understand generative themes of a group as a group participative method | Task 6 | Identifying important sections of reading<br>Recalling examples<br>Creating symbols and representations | ___ Circled relevant section of reading<br>___ Identified example that demonstrated understanding of the method<br>___ Created an appropriate symbol |

EXHIBIT 5.4. ACCOUNTABILITY PLANNER FOR HSERVE 525: SESSION ONE, cont'd.

| SKAs, Content, and Achievement-Based Objectives | Educational Process Elements: Learning Tasks and Materials | Anticipated Changes | Evidence of Change | Documentation of Evidence | Analysis of Evidence |
|---|---|---|---|---|---|
| Knowledge—understand learning needs assessment as a group participative method | Task 7 | | Identifying important sections of reading<br>Recalling examples<br>Identifying personal applications | _____ Circled relevant section of reading<br>_____ Identified example that demonstrated understanding of the method<br>_____ Identified appropriate application | |
| Knowledge—cognitive, affective, and psychomotor aspects of learning | Task 8, lecture; chart: cognitive, affective, psycho-motor aspects; video: health educator | | Listening to a lecture<br>Small-group response questions<br>Writing SNOW cards in small groups | _____ Affirmed understanding of lecture<br>_____ Participated in analysis of video scenario using questions<br>_____ Developed SNOW cards demonstrating understanding | |
| Knowledge—monologue versus dialogue as group participative methods | Task 9 | | Ordering steps in small groups<br>Listening to a monologue<br>Identifying differences with a partner | _____ Participated in small-group activity to put seven steps in order<br>_____ Shared ideas developed with a partner that demonstrated under-standing of differences between monologue and dialogue | |

| | | | | |
|---|---|---|---|---|
| Knowledge—the use of open questions and learning tasks as a group participative method | Task 10, material on open questions | Small-group completion of Open Questions outline | _____ Identified differences in the questions listed in Part 1 <br> _____ Changed a closed question into an open question <br> _____ Designed an effective open question | |
| Skills—developing and using open questions | Task 11 | Identifying situations to use open questions <br> Creating an appropriate question <br> Asking an open-ended question | _____ Identified appropriate situations for open questions <br> _____ Developed an open question appropriate for the situation <br> _____ Reported asking the open question (data collected after Session 1) | |
| Knowledge—the use of feedback <br> Skills—recognition of principles and practices | Task 12, principles and practices, blue cards, evaluation form | Identifying principles and practices demonstrated during the session <br> Completing session evaluation form <br> Sharing celebrations and changes | _____ Accurately selected principles and practices used <br> _____ Completed session evaluation form <br> _____ Actively participated in session feedback | |

designers did not believe the evaluation process demonstrated respect for the learners. They were uncomfortable with observing and listening to learners to verify that the learners were engaged in the process. Nor did they think it necessary to collect information prepared by the students unless it was a specific assignment designed to be submitted for review.

The design team was torn between the time needed for the instructor to focus on the learners' activities and develop accurate records and, alternatively, the inclusion of an observer whose sole purpose was to collect and record the evidence. They felt that an observer would not be considered part of the group and would affect principles of learning such as safety, respect, and inclusion.

Because the program planners did not believe the accountability planner as designed would provide useful information and would interfere with the learning environment of a process already in full swing, they decided that a design using the accountability model but with evidence and documentation procedures more consistent with the philosophy of the School of Public Health would be prepared for session two. The evaluation instrument developed for session one was a self-assessment, a response to a single open question: How has popular education changed your teaching?

Following are the responses of the graduate students, all of them experienced health educators in full-time positions of responsibility around the northwestern United States:

• Popular education has aided me in organizing and structuring my presentations. The skills learned in popular education have kept my topic focus on one important achievement-based objective.

• I developed a prevention workshop for family physicians. I emphasized participants as subjects of their own learning by minimizing the monologue and allowing participants to learn from each other.

• I have contacted learners before class, doing a learning needs assessment. This practice established relationships with group members and set a positive cooperative tone for each session. It jump-starts learning.

• Using the seven steps of planning has helped me to become more confident, organized, and enthusiastic when I do a teaching session. It really helps me think ahead about what I am going to do. It helps me get rid of the fear and jitters.

• Big change! Almost every principle was new to me. Now, I always make sure my teaching includes at least praxis, safety, and needs assessment. In particular, praxis has been valuable in my inpatient teaching of residents. We agree up front to review each patient at discharge and reflect what we did well, what we might have done better, and decide what we will do the next time we are presented with similar circumstances. It is remarkable how often those similar circumstances soon present themselves.

- Popular education has changed my teaching by making me more aware of the learners and their participation in their learning experience. I am more aware of the designs of my lessons and need the time now to practice using the principles that we have learned.
- I learned the value of needs assessment as well as of immediacy and use both in planning classes and in being more flexible with my own agenda. I've learned that a little creativity in presentation and shared learning goes a long way.
- Studying popular education has enlightened me to the power of dialogue rather than monologue in teaching. I find participants more receptive and they seem to learn more quickly when they are engaged and connected and see the relevance of what I am teaching.
- I am used to being a "talking head," lecturing more than using an interactive style in which the learners become partners in the process of learning. I have used the interactive style recently in teaching stress management, giving people a chance to practice various stress management techniques. The feedback was that the learners used several ways to relax and they felt they had more awareness of some techniques they could use in different settings at home or at work.
- Popular education has not changed my teaching, but it has given me a knowledge base that I did not have access to before. Unfortunately, in my situation, I have had to spend a considerable amount of time defending why and how I provide teaching experiences. Popular education has given me a base of theory to draw on.
- I do learning needs assessments prior to every teaching session.
- I am using engagement now that I am aware of how responsive the audience/learners are to active participation. This has made my teaching more fun as well as more meaningful to all participants.
- I rarely do a training now without a learning needs assessment. I am acutely aware of the need for respectful engagement and safety and how tempered my off-the-cuff remarks must be.

Many of the practices described are examples of transfer. And in some instances, as with the praxis work on clinical services, there is significant hope of impact.

## Possible Next Steps

The evaluation experience in this case study demonstrates the difficulty of "backing in" to evaluation. Materials that had already been developed for the first course session were designed to accomplish specific learning tasks developed from identified achievement-based objectives. It was anticipated by the course developers that the learners would accomplish each learning task and could measure their success through self-assessment as well as future planning and practice opportunities assigned to each student. The self-assessment is shown in Exhibit 5.5.

## EXHIBIT 5.5.  END-OF-COURSE SELF-ASSESSMENT FOR HSERVE 525.

A force field evaluation manifests the strengths and the weaknesses of a program, in this case from the perception of the learners.

|  | Liked | Suggestions for Changes |
| --- | --- | --- |
| *Structure or Design*<br>Readings (nontextbook) |  |  |
| Teaching: How popular<br>education was modeled |  |  |
| Opportunity for and type of<br>feedback from instructors:<br>  Written<br>  Oral |  |  |
| Amount of outside work |  |  |
| *Class*<br>Length of sessions |  |  |
| Meeting times |  |  |
| Social time added to class |  |  |
| Location (physical space) |  |  |
| Food for social times |  |  |
| *Staff*<br>Performance of staff:<br>  Trez<br>  Maureen<br>  Bob<br>  Karen |  |  |
| *Materials*<br>Book (text) |  |  |

Would you be interested in an opportunity for periodic support of your efforts in popular health education? If yes, check what form that support should take.

☐ Quarterly optional meetings of past and present popular education students to share ideas

☐ Phone access for technical assistance

☐ Web sites for popular education

☐ Dialogue via e-mail

Other suggestions:

One possibility is that the organization may be satisfied with the design and not have significant concerns about the need to document results. Program instructors interact regularly with learners during the extended program and have many opportunities for qualitative feedback. Unless other stakeholders have concerns that are not addressed by available information, additional evaluation may not be necessary to meet the needs of program planners.

However, if the program is being redesigned there are opportunities to develop learning activities and evaluation procedures within the new design that are more compatible with the philosophy of the program planners. Examples to guide that type of redesign effort are included in Chapter Six, which shows a redesign of a course under the influence of the accountability planner. The planners may want to incorporate more specific self-assessments, like the one in Exhibit 5.5, and diverse forms of feedback as well as a variety of activities for which the results are tangible evidence of the SKAs on which the training is focused. Since this is a health education methods course, the modeling of this evaluation process is very important.

Another strategy would involve additional work between the evaluation planners and the University of Washington course designers. Close collaboration to clarify language, match objectives more specifically with learning tasks and data collection alternatives, and consider alternative and unobtrusive information sources and data collection methods may result in an accepted and useable accountability planner. Recognition that an objective and specific evaluation procedure is compatible with the principles and practices of popular education may encourage program planners to include more evaluation elements.

This case shows a university situation where professors and instructors were open to the innovative recognition of evaluation as collaboration between staff and students, among staff, and among students.

## Case Three: LVA's Training of Trainers Workshop

In January 1994 Jubilee provided week-long training to Literacy Volunteers of America (LVA) leadership personnel who were searching for a new approach to training. In the past three years Jubilee, in conference events and in national training of volunteer leaders, has been closely involved with LVA in the design of its new materials.

Literacy Volunteers of America is a national organization with state-level support for local affiliates. The criteria for approving a local volunteer literacy provider as a member organization include agreeing to use LVA-approved tutor training in Basic Literacy or English as a Second Language (ESL) as the core of its program and carrying out management standards as detailed in LVA's *50/50 Management* text. LVA has an approach to helping adults learn that is collaborative and student centered.

## The Education Program

Literacy Volunteers of America offers programs and materials to assist in the development of volunteer tutors for basic literacy programs and programs that teach English as a second language through local organizations. To ensure the effectiveness of the training program, a workshop called Training of Trainers was designed to teach prospective tutor trainers how to use principles of popular education. A two-day, twelve-hour class was planned and structured through a comprehensive facilitator's guide. The *LVA Guide for Training Tutors* includes an outline of the workshop developed around specific learning tasks. For each learning task, basic directions, scripts, background information, and teaching suggestions are provided in an easy-to-use format. In addition to the teaching outline, the guide includes a preworkshop participant's packet, lists of needed materials and supplies, and prepared masters for paper charts and overhead transparencies. Formative and end-of-workshop evaluation procedures are also provided.

## The LVA Accountability Planner

Using the accountability planner design and the *LVA Guide for Training Tutors,* a comprehensive evaluation plan to be used in the local workshops was prepared. The lead author of the guide and a Jubilee Fellow, Chloe Fessler, reviewed the accountability planner and provided extensive feedback. Using that review, a revised planner was prepared, a brief section of which is shown in Exhibit 5.6. As with the University of Washington accountability planner, certain columns could not be completed because the planner was based on an existing program plan that did not specifically consider the named evaluation elements.

A second accountability planner was developed for the LVA case because of the specific thinking and planning completed by the organization. Because of the relationship between the national organization and the local affiliates who use the materials and managerial support of LVA, clear and specific outcomes for the tutor training program have been specified as well as organizational performance expectations. This detailed planning provides the opportunity to look at transfer and impact measures in a way not possible with many other programs.

Because LVA did not connect transfer and impact outcomes to specific sections of the program, a complete six-column accountability planner cannot be illustrated. However, the two columns shown in Exhibit 5.7 correspond to columns

**EXHIBIT 5.6. THE LVA ACCOUNTABILITY PLANNER.**

| SKAs, Content, and Achievement-Based Objectives | Educational Process Elements: Learning Tasks and Materials | Anticipated Changes | Evidence of Change | Documentation of Evidence | Analysis of Evidence |
|---|---|---|---|---|---|
| Skills—use *cloze* activities (in which reader supplies missing words) as context clues to increase learners' reading fluency and text comprehension | Materials: Chart 3.1, *Tutor* pages 57–58<br>Tasks: group practice | Group responses in practice session | | ___ Participants completed Session 3<br><br>___ Participants used cloze activities as context clues during group practice | |
| Skills—use the phonics technique when appropriate to teach letter-sound relationships | Materials: LVA phonics tape, Video 4, Overhead 3.2, Learning task 3.2, *Tutor* pages 60–63 and 169<br>Tasks: trainer presentation, listen and respond verbally to audiotape, view video, group discussion, trainer demonstration, paired work | Follow steps of the technique on pages 60–63 of *Tutor*<br><br>Homework—written statement on the phonics technique and its use in a lesson | | ___ Participants followed steps of the technique during paired practice<br><br>___ Participants developed written statements on the phonics technique | |
| Skills—use the word pattern technique to increase independent reading proficiency of learners | Materials: Handout 3.2, Video 4, *Tutor* pages 66, 68, 73, 169, 180, Overhead 3.3–3.4, Learning task 3.3, Chart 3.2<br>Tasks: Trainer presentation, view video, group discussion, trainer demonstration, paired practice, small group demonstration | Follow guide on page 68 of *Tutor*<br><br>Homework—written statement on the word pattern technique and its use in a lesson | | ___ Participants demonstrated when and how to use the phonics technique during practice<br><br>___ Participants followed the guide during paired practice<br><br>___ Participants demonstrated when and how to use the word pattern during practice | |

# EXHIBIT 5.7. TRANSFER AND IMPACT IN LVA TUTOR TRAINING

Instructions: The following pages were developed to determine the changes that occur over an extended period of time as a result of using the trainer's guide for a number of workshops. Information should be collected prior to offering workshops using the trainer's guide and then regularly every three to six months thereafter, in order to compare evidence collected. The anticipated changes listed in the left column have been identified by LVA as important outcomes of LVA Tutor Training.

| ANTICIPATED CHANGE (organization, job, learner) | EVIDENCE OF CHANGE |
|---|---|
| Volunteers who can manage local programs in Basic Literacy and English as a Second Language (learner) | _____ Number of volunteers who completed the training program who have become local program managers |
| Volunteers who can tutor adults and teens to read, write, understand, and speak English (learner) | _____ Number of volunteers who have completed the training program and can be assigned as tutors |
| Volunteers who use learner-centered instruction and real-world materials in promoting literacy (learner) | _____ Number of tutors who have provided evidence they can use learner-centered instruction regularly as a part of tutoring activities |
| LVA Basic Literacy Tutor Training Workshops will be participatory and based on adult learning theory (job) | _____ Number of LVA Tutor Training Workshops that documented the use of participatory and learner-centered strategies identified in the Trainer's Guide |
| LVA Workshops will be conducted by training teams (job) | _____ Number of LVA Tutor Training Workshops conducted by training teams |
| Local affiliate organizations will build a long-term commitment to a continuing education process (organization) | _____ Number of local affiliates that have provided evidence of a continuing education process |
| Local affiliate organizations will provide continuing support for tutors (organization) | _____ Number of local affiliates who have provided evidence of continuing tutor support |
| **Workshop Impact** | |
| Effectively reduce the dropout rate in tutor training programs | _____ Change in dropout rates before and after using revised materials |
| Tutors who are better matched to learners | _____ Change in number of reported mismatches before and after using revised materials |
| More effective tutors | _____ Improvement in evaluations completed on tutors by learners and mentors before and after using the revised materials |
| More effective recruitment of volunteers for positions other than tutors | _____ Change in the number of volunteers recruited for nontutor positions before and after using the revised materials |
| **Learner-Centered Literacy Education Impact** | |
| Learners with ability to read and write | _____ Improvement in number of learners successfully developing the ability to read and write as a result of tutoring |
| Increased personal freedom of learners | _____ Improvement in learner attitudes and experiences related to their personal freedoms compared to those of others not completing literacy tutoring |
| Maintenance of a democratic society | _____ Improvement in learner attitudes and participation in democratic institutions and activities with others not completing literacy tutoring |

three and four in a usual accountability planner. You can see how columns five and six can be developed by identifying where the information is available in the local organizations, determining when the information should be collected and reported and who has the responsibility for data collection, and making the comparisons suggested to determine the effect of the revised program on specified outcomes.

## Using the Evaluation Results

The LVA case provides the most comprehensive program plan incorporating specific popular education planning elements with precise SKAs, learning tasks, and evaluation strategies. Even though the accountability planner was developed after program planning was complete, there was a good match among the elements. When information needed to complete the planner was missing, discussions between the evaluation planners and the program planners resolved the problem.

Most importantly, the careful development of long-term outcome statements shows how a carefully planned education and training program can make a difference in the organization that uses the program. When an organization can point to improved job performance and significant changes in the people who are affected by the organization, the value of the education and training efforts is clear.

In the case of LVA, the transfer and impact results that were identified can be determined through records maintained and reported by local affiliates. The results, if positive, should strengthen the relationships between the national and local organization and be very important information to share with LVA stakeholders and the communities in which the local organizations are working to increase literacy.

From the viewpoint of Jubilee, the evidence collected by LVA provides a direct measure of the use and usefulness of popular education principles. By evaluating the revised training guide prepared under the direction of a Jubilee Fellow, evidence became clear of the ability of a program completer to use the principles and practices on the job. Further, the reach and impact of Jubilee moves beyond the Fellows who complete the Jubilee courses as organizations like LVA provide Jubilee with objective evidence that popular education practices are being used in hundreds of local literacy programs throughout the United States and Canada.

## Possible Next Steps

As with the previous cases, LVA can continue to refine the evaluation process in future revisions of the training program with precise matches between all elements of the program and by identifying additional efficient and effective ways to collect evaluation information. LVA in particular is in a position to collect and analyze data from a number of programs over an extended period of time and develop an evaluation data base. With the large amount of data, the organization can look for patterns and trends and make objective determinations of program elements that are particularly effective or in need of further revision.

In the three case studies in this chapter the Jubilee approach was designed into the programs and the evaluation process came later. In Chapter Six we examine the Jubilee Introduction to Popular Education course as it has been reexamined and redesigned using the accountability planner.

# EVALUATION AND ACCOUNTABILITY AT JUBILEE TODAY

I n this chapter we use the accountability process and planner on the five-day intensive course called Learning to Listen, Learning to Teach: Introduction to Popular Education. Chapter One describes how the research done for this book has affected how we do needs assessment and how and what we teach about evaluation theory and practice. Chapter Three shows how the accountability planner can be used to examine what the course design reflects of intention toward impact. Here we review the use of the accountability process and planner on a selection of content and achievement-based objectives. Remember, the content in the seven steps of planning is the *what*; the achievement-based objectives are the *what for*. Because these were carefully laid out already, using the accountability planner became for us the continuation of a planning process.

Following are all the achievement-based objectives (ABOs) of the present course. In Chapter Two you saw how to use the accountability process to evaluate the learning, transfer, and impact of one content piece: using open questions. In Chapter Three you worked through the accountability planner on the achievement-based objective of identifying a group's generative themes. Now we will design an accountability planner to work through three more course objectives and content pieces. The Appendix gives a complete accountability planner for the Introduction to Popular Education course.

By the end of this five-day course, all participants will have done the following:

*ABOs of the Introduction to Popular Education Course*

1. *Reviewed* current adult learning theory
2. *Distinguished* between monologue (banking) and dialogue (problem posing) as approaches to learning (the Freire concept)
3. *Reviewed* basic communications theory using the Eric Berne paradigm (transactional analysis: Parent, Adult, Child)
4. *Practiced* doing a learning needs assessment
5. *Identified* the generative themes of a group
6. *Practiced* working in small groups
7. *Examined* a theory of how groups work
8. *Practiced* designing and using open questions
9. *Identified* and *practiced* using the seven steps of planning
10. *Reviewed* and *used* the concept of ideas, feelings, and actions in learning
11. *Examined* and *practiced* using all of the principles and practices of popular education
12. *Practiced* designing learning sessions in teams (meetings, courses, workshops, orientation programs, training sessions) using the principles and practices of popular education
13. *Examined* video clips and *identified* ways to use them effectively
14. *Designed* an effective chart and *named* the qualities of effective charts
15. *Practiced* teaching using their design
16. *Practiced* learning as subjects (decision makers) of their own learning
17. *Reviewed* theory on feedback; *practiced* giving and getting feedback on designs and teaching
18. *Examined* a model for planning (the four I's)
19. *Named* resources in popular education: books, journals, professional organizations, courses

The accountability planner enables examination of the congruence and consistency of a program design. Completing the planner's columns before delivering the program makes it possible to discover where the gaps are, whether the tasks that lead to achieving the objectives are complete or incomplete, and whether the materials might be inappropriate or inadequate to the job.

The inevitable question: Is this process planning or evaluation? Our inevitable response: Yes!

Exhibit 6.1 shows the portion of the Introduction to Popular Education course's accountability planner that has to do with how adults learn. Note that there is constant iteration of means of analysis and documentation. Once you start using this instrument, you see that one analysis task is to look in many places for many diverse bits of evidence. As you review the rest of the planner, watch for this iteration.

**EXHIBIT 6.1. THE ACCOUNTABILITY PLANNER: HOW ADULTS LEARN.**

| Column 1 | Column 2 | Column 3 | Column 4 | Column 5 | Column 6 |
|---|---|---|---|---|---|
| SKAs, Content, and Achievement-Based Objectives | Educational Process Elements: Learning Tasks and Materials | Anticipated Changes • Learning • Transfer • Impact | Evidence of Change • Content • Process • Qualitative • Quantitative | Documentation of Evidence | Analysis of Evidence |
| 1. Reviewed current adult learning theory | *Learning Tasks 3, 11, 20*<br><br>Learning task 3: how adults learn<br><br>3A. In pairs, describe the best learning situation in your life. Then analyze it. What factors made it so good? Write these factors on SNOW cards, one on a card. We'll share all of them and then compare our factors with current research on adult learning.<br><br>Chart 3: how adults learn<br><br>*Our Factors*<br>Chart 3A: how adults learn (Knowles, 1980)<br>1. Respect<br>2. Immediacy<br>3. Relevance<br>4. 20 percent of what we hear<br>40 percent of what we see and hear<br>80 percent of what we do | *Learning*<br>Participants will<br>1. Show respect to one another<br>2. Consider immediacy of content: to learners when they design<br>3. Select topics for microteaching that are relevant to this group<br>4. Design and use learning tasks so the learners do what they are learning<br><br>Participants use learning tasks to teach, demonstrating the Lewin principle that learning is more effective when it is active rather than passive.<br><br>Participants will examine teaching designs for cognitive, affective, and psychomotor aspects, demonstrating the Lewin principle. | *Learning*<br>Participants<br>1. Show respect to one another<br>2. Consider immediacy of content to learners when they design<br>3. Select topics for microteaching that are relevant to this group<br>4. Design and use learning tasks so what they are learning<br><br>Participants use learning tasks to teach, demonstrating the Lewin principle that learning is more effective when it is active rather than passive.<br><br>Participants examine teaching designs for cognitive, affective, and psychomotor aspects, demonstrating the Lewin principle. | *Learning*<br>Videotapes of the learning designs are examined to note specific examples of respect.<br><br>A videotape of a day at the course shows small groups with learners constantly engaged: observers can count the times individual speak. Records of comprehensive responses to learning tasks throughout the course show that everyone has something to offer.<br><br>The videos of the second designs note changes in the learning designs to implement feedback on learning tasks, small-group work, the need for more affective and psychomotor activity, and the need to echo and paraphrase in active listening. | *Learning*<br>These videotapes are reviewed by other teams during day five; they are sent to Jubilee Associates for review by Jubilee Associates after the course. In those reviews we refer constantly to the four concepts: respect, immediacy, relevance, and doing. |

# EXHIBIT 6.1. THE ACCOUNTABILITY PLANNER: HOW ADULTS LEARN, cont'd.

| Column 1 | Column 2 | Column 3 | Column 4 | Column 5 | Column 6 |
|---|---|---|---|---|---|
| SKAs, Content, and Achievement-Based Objectives | Educational Process Elements: Learning Tasks and Materials | Anticipated Changes<br>• Learning<br>• Transfer<br>• Impact | Evidence of Change<br>• Content<br>• Process<br>• Qualitative<br>• Quantitative | Documentation of Evidence | Analysis of Evidence |
| | Task 11: Lewin's Dozen (Johnson and Johnson, 1991)<br><br>11A. Listen to this summary of the life and work of Kurt Lewin.<br><br>11B. Each person select one number. Please read your principle for the whole group.<br><br>11C. At your table, study that single principle of Lewin; then do the practical application questions on that page with the others in your small group.<br><br>11D. Listen as all participants read their principle again in turn. What similarities do you notice among them all? Tell one way Lewin's principles will help you when you begin to design and teach. | Participants will use small groups in their teaching designs, demonstrating Lewin's principles about the power of small groups.<br><br><br><br><br><br><br><br><br><br><br><br><br><br><br><br><br><br>*Transfer*<br>Participants use the four concepts just listed and Lewin's dozen principles as they design training on the job. | Participants use small groups in their teaching designs, demonstrating Lewin's principles about the power of small groups.<br><br><br><br><br><br><br><br>*Transfer*<br>They use these four concepts and Lewin's dozen principles as they design training on the job.<br><br>*Impact*<br>Their organizations begin to use these four concepts and twelve principles in meetings, training sessions, orientation, and so on. They use this language: active learners, respect, immediacy, and relevance throughout the organization. | *Transfer*<br>These designs are collected in a portfolio in chronological order and show growing use of the principles of adult learning.<br><br>*Impact*<br>The culture of the organization changes into that of a learning, listening organization. There is a new vigor and spontaneity among employees and 30 percent less turnover. | *Transfer*<br>Jubilee does a monthly review of the designs sent in, with reports going back to participants and their supervisors showing on a five-point scale the creativity and consistency of these designs in terms of adult learning theory.<br><br>*Impact*<br>The organization is celebrated as a prominent learning organization by a national review board. Its funding increases by 20 percent.<br><br>Checklist for particular aspects of theory:<br>Respect<br>Immediacy<br>Relevance<br>CAP: cognitive, affective, psychomotor 80 percent do |

| Task 20: Design | Impact | | |
|---|---|---|---|
| 20A. Select one other person to make up a team of two to design and do practice teaching. Decide what you want to teach about. Select a topic that you feel strongly about. Decide whose topic will be designed and taught first.<br><br>20B. Design and do a learning needs assessment with this group on the first topic.<br><br>20C. Use the seven steps of planning and all the principles and practices to design learning tasks and problem-posing learning materials for a forty-minute session. You will design and teach for both topics together, as a team. | *Impact*<br>Their organizations will begin to use these four concepts and twelve principles in meetings, training sessions, orientations, and so on. They will use this language: active learners, respect, immediacy, and relevance throughout the organization. | | |

Note in Exhibit 6.2 that it is not always possible to anticipate how evidence will emerge for transfer or impact variables. A conservative approach is appropriate here, but using the accountability planner in this case makes it possible for us to categorize the data that *are* received from Jubilee Fellows about the growing success of their work and increasing ease of teamwork. We do have to be cautious not to project our hopefulness on the data, however.

Sometimes only the learning section of the planner is used in advance of the course, with the transfer and impact sections done afterward; see Exhibit 6.3.

In honoring course participants as subjects of their own work, trainers can still make suggestions on application; ultimately, however, the participants have the deliberative voice on how they will use what they have learned in their workplace—how they transfer it, in other words (see Exhibit 6.4). Their autonomy can make them more accountable to their organizations.

In Exhibit 6.5, note that we use different means of measurement in column six, analysis of documentation: a checklist, a scale, incidents in a session, peer review using the checklist. Your job is to design accessible and valid instruments of analysis that will prove to you and to the learners that they are doing what they learned.

How does one *do*—that is, carry out—a concept? That is where learning tasks come in. One of the most important axioms of popular education as defined by Jubilee is that a learning task is a task for the learner! What about *doing* in terms of teaching attitudes? Remember that attitudes are caught, not taught. Using the accountability model in your planning can be very effective in teaching others the respectful aspects of assiduous preparation, because you will clearly have done careful planning.

Chapter Three offers analytical questions to examine how well and how often learners do something with the concept of generative themes. The attitude of respect, for example, can be measured in a video by citing how often the teacher uses language that is respectful in that context. We can cite in the video how well and how often the teacher affirms and paraphrases contributions, which is a universal mode of respect.

Notice that people use diverse modes of proof. Chapter Two gives the example of teaching how to recognize design and use open questions; Chapter Three shows a graduated example of the use of the accountability planner on the content piece of generative themes; and here we show use of the planner to reconsider the design of the entire Jubilee Introduction to Popular Education course. The observer is part of what she observes. According to that axiom, our idiosyncratic and personal preferences in measurement may favor qualitative measures over quantitative, surveys over interviews, peer analysis over supervisor review—or the opposite.

The point is not to have a tight set of techniques exactly matching learning task to technique, but to realize at the outset that what we are teaching will have

**EXHIBIT 6.2. THE ACCOUNTABILITY PLANNER: MONOLOGUE AND DIALOGUE.**

| Column 1 | Column 2 | Column 3 | Column 4 | Column 5 | Column 6 |
|---|---|---|---|---|---|
| SKAs, Content, and Achievement-Based Objectives | Educational Process Elements: Learning Tasks and Materials | Anticipated Changes<br>• Learning<br>• Transfer<br>• Impact | Evidence of Change<br>• Content<br>• Process<br>• Qualitative<br>• Quantitative | Documentation of Evidence | Analysis of Evidence |
| 2. Distinguished between monologue and dialogue | Learning task 6: Identify the differences between monologue and dialogue after an experience with both<br><br>21. Design using dialogue<br><br>25. Design using dialogue again, after receiving feedback | *Learning*<br>Participants name observed differences between monologue and dialogue.<br><br>*Transfer*<br>They design for dialogue when teaching.<br><br>*Impact*<br>Courses are consistently designed for dialogue. | *Learning*<br>They list differences between monologue and dialogue. Questions in course report about lectures as monologue.<br><br>*Transfer*<br>Designs from these participants, reviewed by Jubilee, show use of learning tasks.<br><br>*Impact*<br>Course outlines show learning tasks that invite dialogue. | *Learning*<br>List of differences<br>List of their questions in the report<br><br>*Transfer*<br>Their designs<br><br>*Impact*<br>The course plans and outlines used in their organization | *Learning*<br>The list is comprehensive in terms of their experience: practical not academic.<br><br>All questions show concern for teaching a mass of material.<br><br>*Transfer*<br>Peer review using the Jubilee checklist Building a portfolio for use in the Jubilee cluster group meeting<br><br>*Impact*<br>Engaged learners sell courses, so registration numbers are up. |

# EXHIBIT 6.3. THE ACCOUNTABILITY PLANNER: BERNE'S COMMUNICATIONS THEORY.

| Column 1 | Column 2 | Column 3 | Column 4 | Column 5 | Column 6 |
|---|---|---|---|---|---|
| **SKAs, Content, and Achievement-Based Objectives** | **Educational Process Elements: Learning Tasks and Materials** | **Anticipated Changes**<br>• **Learning**<br>• **Transfer**<br>• **Impact** | **Evidence of Change**<br>• **Content**<br>• **Process**<br>• **Qualitative**<br>• **Quantitative** | **Documentation of Evidence** | **Analysis of Evidence** |
| 3. Reviewed basic communications theory using the Eric Berne paradigm of transactional analysis: parent, adult, child | Learning Task 12: communications theory: parent, adult, child (Berne)<br><br>12A. Listen to this story: "My Sister."<br><br>12B. Read this brief description of Berne's theory.<br><br>12C. Listen to this illustrated lecture on Berne's theory. What are your questions?<br><br>12D. Identify verbs that you associate with any one of the ego states.<br><br>12E. In pairs, name what ego states you saw yourself in since you woke this morning. | *Learning*<br>Participants will use the language of transactional analysis in planning, working in teams, and giving feedback. | *Learning*<br>TA language use<br><br>Conflict resolution<br><br>Teamwork flows well<br><br>Action style: Participants stop and think and are quiet before speaking. | *Learning*<br>Videos of their teaching practice<br><br>Their feedback responses to the course<br><br>Anecdotes from their teamwork | *Learning*<br>Checklist of adult-adult transactions in their teaching<br><br>Their use of TA language in their feedback |

**EXHIBIT 6.4. THE ACCOUNTABILITY PLANNER: HOW GROUPS WORK.**

| Column 1 | Column 2 | Column 3 | Column 4 | Column 5 | Column 6 |
|---|---|---|---|---|---|
| **SKAs, Content, and Achievement-Based Objectives** | **Educational Process Elements: Learning Tasks and Materials** | **Anticipated Changes**<br>• Learning<br>• Transfer<br>• Impact | **Evidence of Change**<br>• Content<br>• Process<br>• Qualitative<br>• Quantitative | **Documentation of Evidence** | **Analysis of Evidence** |
| 7. Examined a theory of effective group work | Learning task 17 | *Learning*<br>They will use this theory in their own small-group work.<br><br>*Transfer*<br>They will use this in daily work, checking on all group and task maintenance roles.<br><br>*Impact*<br>More team planning of training | *Learning*<br>They refer to the bicycle as a metaphor for their group and task maintenance.<br><br>*Transfer*<br>Their planning is more often done in teams.<br><br>*Impact*<br>Enthusiasm, fun during planning | *Learning*<br>Anecdotes<br>Reports of how the planning went<br><br>*Transfer*<br>Team designs submitted for review<br><br>*Impact*<br>Quality of work<br>Quantity of work | *Learning*<br>Peer review<br>Self-review: how we did planning as a team, using the checklist of group and task skills<br><br>*Transfer*<br>Checklist for all roles—who did what?<br><br>*Impact*<br>Fewer conflict situations during planning |

# EXHIBIT 6.5. THE ACCOUNTABILITY PLANNER: SEVEN STEPS OF PLANNING.

| Column 1<br><br>SKAs, Content, and Achievement-Based Objectives | Column 2<br><br>Educational Process Elements: Learning Tasks and Materials | Column 3<br><br>Anticipated Changes<br>• Learning<br>• Transfer<br>• Impact | Column 4<br><br>Evidence of Change<br>• Content<br>• Process<br>• Qualitative<br>• Quantitative | Column 5<br><br>Documentation of Evidence | Column 6<br><br>Analysis of Evidence |
|---|---|---|---|---|---|
| 9. Identified and practiced use of the seven steps of planning | Learning task 6: monologue and dialogue<br><br>16. Designing Together<br><br>20, 24. Design | *Learning*<br>Participants will use the seven steps every time they design.<br><br>*Transfer*<br>They will use the seven steps in planning on their job.<br><br>*Impact*<br>Who: Training will be more appropriate for the selected group. What, when: Trainers will not try to do too much in the allotted time so the educational potential is higher. What, what for: Training is more specific and detailed. How: Trainers do not rush to the *how* but are more intentional (this is both a transfer and an impact indicator). | *Learning*<br>They argue about the order of the seven steps, offering cogent reasons for their sequence.<br><br>They refer to the seven steps in the Designing Together task for the AIDS hotline. They pull out the seven steps cards to begin their planning.<br><br>*Transfer*<br>The seven steps cards are visible and the steps are used in designs shown to Jubilee for review.<br><br>*Impact*<br>Designs of training are more intentional and reasonable in terms of time, content, and continuity because the organizations are using the seven steps. | *Learning*<br>Their designs show the use of the seven steps.<br><br>Their designs show when they did *not* use a particular step.<br><br>*Transfer*<br>Those designs<br><br>*Impact*<br>Those designs Meetings plans Gatherings and conference designs | *Learning*<br>All steps used? Some steps omitted?<br><br>*Transfer*<br>Designs submitted from the work site to Jubilee are examined for comprehensive use of the seven steps.<br><br>*Impact*<br>Reviewed for the use of the seven steps |

results in action and behavior, ways of thinking and attitudes, and that the developmental aspects can be measured. Once we think that way, the hard work of completing the accountability planner when designing with the seven steps will be motivated by our own passion for excellence in teaching and learning.

Note also that it is not necessary to fill in all the blanks: If you do not know how to respond, do not respond. Perhaps the learners will help you or responses will arise as you begin to think this way about your teaching and their learning. How do they know they know? is not a question that deserves a facile answer; it is a big question that leads to other big questions.

CHAPTER SEVEN

# REFLECTIONS AND NEXT STEPS

We have come to the end of a most interesting journey toward creating a useful evaluation process for practitioners who do adult education. The journey began as an attempt to more fully answer the question posed in *Learning to Listen, Learning to Teach*, one that Jubilee Fellows also often ask: How do they know they know? In other words, how can we know that programs integrating the principles and practices of popular education are effective? We have tried to present an accountable process of evaluation that is at once accessible and respectful of both the organization and the people participating in the evaluation process.

Each of the coauthors of this book has grown through the writing process as we challenged principles and philosophies during our constant dialogue, refined the procedures through interactions with the case study organizations, and wrote and rewrote each page of the manuscript. In this final chapter we offer our reflections on the accountability process as we now see it, and on those evaluation principles and philosophy that continue to guide our work.

## Who Should Use This Accountability Model and When?

Educators generally recognize that determining how participants have benefited from the experience is a vital part of the learning process for the learners themselves. Therefore, some form of formal or informal assessment or feedback for learners is included in most program designs. In the same way, most educators agree that they must determine whether a program has been well designed and proven effective. However, specific efforts to gather information competent to answer those qualitative questions are rare.

Many reasons can be given for the limited attention paid to the planning of evaluation. Some common reasons are the generally narrow and negative perceptions people hold about evaluation, the limited time and resources available to support educational programming resulting in the decision to eliminate or minimize evaluation, the concern that evaluation activities will detract from the cooperative climate and the adult learning experience, and the feeling that evaluation results will be misinterpreted, misused, or identify weaknesses in a program design.

Each organization must decide whether evaluation can be a part of the programming procedure. Externally imposed evaluation or evaluation that is not supported and accepted by people in the organization will have little value in accomplishing its primary purpose, which is to improve the education process by determining how well anticipated outcomes are achieved. Evaluation procedures and results that do not contribute to that purpose are of no value.

Much can be learned about the commitment of an organization to its mission and goals by studying the procedures used and resources committed to education. Haphazard or incomplete programming or the allocation of inadequate resources to effectively implement education initiatives reduces the likelihood of the organization's success. Those organizations willing to carefully plan, reasonably support, and objectively evaluate education efforts directed at accomplishing important goals are making an important statement about those goals.

There are many ways to complete program evaluations and a variety of elements to evaluate. We suggest that an organization committed to evaluation can and should control the evaluation process and determine what is to be evaluated. Those decisions should be made carefully and objectively. They should be made with the participation of all important stakeholders in the program (learners, organizations that send the learners or will benefit from the learners' knowledge and skills after the program, funding agencies, and the like). If external organizations require evaluation of an adult education program, they must be held accountable to make evaluation objectives clear from the beginning. They must involve the program planners and other stakeholders in the evaluation planning process.

## Why Evaluate?

As program evaluators with experience in a variety of organizations and many types of education and training programs, we continually see specific benefits from well-planned evaluation efforts. As we highlight them here, we ask you to consider where you have seen similar results or indeed are able to identify other benefits.

*Evaluation informs.* Evaluation results inform us about achievement of objectives and development of learner SKAs. We can know if our efforts are having the desired effect. It informs learners of their progress during the program and improvements in their capabilities when they finish the program and return to their work or daily lives. Organizations are informed about the improvements that can be expected as a result of the education or training program and the value received as a result of their support of the program.

*Evaluation improves.* Evaluation improves decision making because future decisions can be based on experience and results. Program elements that clearly work can be retained; those that do not can be modified. SKAs that make a difference in learner performance can continue to be emphasized while those that make little or no contribution can be deemphasized or eliminated.

*Evaluation increases confidence.* Nothing reinforces a learner's commitment to a learning experience more than evidence that it will result in improved knowledge or performance. In the same way, program designers and instructors are encouraged by information demonstrating that their decisions and work had the desired effect. People who have a stake in the program or work with those who complete the program will benefit from objective evidence that the program has made a difference.

*Evaluation enhances education.* The willingness of educators to subject their work to assessment demonstrates confidence in that work. Clearly stating expected outcomes and objectively determining if those objectives are achieved demonstrates to others that there is a system and science to educational practice. It shows we are serious about our work and committed to best practice.

## Using Evaluation Results

If evaluation results are not utilized they are of no value. As we work with organizations to prepare the accountability planner that is the planning document for the accountability process we are often asked, "Why go to all this trouble? How will we use all the information we obtain?" These are very important questions that should guide evaluation planning.

In Chapter Five we provided examples that demonstrate that every achievement-based objective and individual SKA in a program can be evaluated. We saw how three organizations used the accountability planner to evaluate programs, even though those programs were already in operation. Chapter Six and the Appendix show an accountability planner that responded to each of the objectives in the Jubilee introductory course. This comprehensive evaluation of all objectives was, for Jubilee, a template laid over the program so that our redesign had fewer gaps and omissions.

We want to reinforce the importance of selecting for evaluation only those elements of a program about which decision makers and stakeholders want information. We never want to overwhelm the organization or the process with information; evaluation is designed to improve the program, not burden it. Evaluation results can provide information on critical program outcomes and elements. In this way, the importance of the organization and its stakeholders as owners of the evaluation process is reinforced.

Evaluation results have specific short-term and long-term benefits. In the short run (while the program is going on and immediately at its conclusion), evidence of learner achievement is an important evaluation result. By gathering information on learner performance (skills, knowledge, and attitudes), judgments can be made about which outcomes have been achieved and which need additional attention. Comparing learner performance results with their capabilities before participating in the program will show which of the outcomes were most effectively developed during the program. Comparing learner performance with that of others not in the program demonstrates the value of the education experience. Setting predetermined standards and measuring learner performance against those standards shows whether the program can accomplish the desired results.

The short-term effectiveness of specific program elements and activities can also be determined while the program is under way and at its end. Evaluation of program elements can provide evidence that an activity had the desired result, that learners who completed the activity benefited while other learners did not, or that the element or activity was completed in the way planned. In that way, program planners can judge whether to retain the activity, make changes, or find ways to strengthen relationships among program elements.

In the long run, program evaluators can collect information to determine if the program resulted in improved performance well after the program is completed. Specifically, if a program is effective, we should be able to see learners doing things in different and better ways after the program than before or when compared to similar individuals who have not completed the program. Organizations that have committed to the program by sponsoring it or sending learners to it need to see evidence of results. Comparisons can be made using important organizational performance information collected before participating in the program or with similar organizations that have not been involved in the experience.

One of the most enlightening benefits of long-term evaluation comes when we can observe the result learners are achieving in their own work. This is what we mean by impact. Who do learners touch? What are the benefits from the work of learners who completed the program? Consider the excitement in Jubilee when we receive evidence from all over the world of learners who are active participants and increasingly autonomous in their learning because they participate in experiences designed and delivered by Jubilee Fellows and Jubilee Associates. What better evidence of the achievement of the mission of an organization?

## Further Reflections

One message we hope you take away after reading and working through this book is that evaluation is about choices and collaboration. You as the designer and evaluator are the subject, decision maker, and pilot of the process. You decide, as did our colleagues at the University of Washington, NETWORK, and LVA, how to best use the accountability process in your context. Those who are external to your program cannot know what you know; therefore, you are the judge of your own work. Others make judgments against criteria you have set. Your likelihood of success is increased when evaluation is designed and conducted in concert with the learners, who are themselves subjects of their own learning. We hope you now have a new perspective on evaluation: a positive sense that the accountability process is one of enhancement and not of correction.

Two of the authors frequently work as consultants to improve educational efforts in industry, where evaluation is often used with a primary focus on performance-based training. In designing such training, evaluators draw heavily on the goals and needs of the organization. Two items, outcomes (can the trainee perform?) and results (did the investment in training directly help the organization achieve its objectives?), get significant evaluation attention. In such situations evaluators often spend less time on process.

In writing this book we have seen again the importance of that process, captured in the principles and practices of popular education. We see anew how outcomes are influenced by the ways we design and deliver education and training. Conversely, the need stands to identify objective measures in the design of education programs and to look for evidence of those results as an indication of program effectiveness. We have once more been reminded to hold the opposites! Through our collaboration and partnership, both process and product are richer.

## Postscript

### Jane Vella

During the preparation of this book, in the research and writing, I was often the learner; I peppered Jim Burrow and Paula Berardinelli with questions and demanded clarification of their language and reasons for their decisions. Throughout, I had unorthodox feelings: "Why all this trouble? I am a good teacher. The learners respond enthusiastically to the courses Jubilee designs and leads. Why all this demand for specific data about learning, transfer, and impact?" My colleagues patiently, consistently responded from their wide experience in the industrial sector, "Industry cannot spend millions of dollars on training without solid assurance of value added." The baggage manager at the airport has got to have the *skills* to recognize a suspicious piece of cargo; the physician's assistant in a clinic has got to have the *knowledge* to diagnose a faulty pregnancy; the engineer at NASA has got to have the *attitude* of courage to confront administrators who want to send the spacecraft off in bad weather. As you see, the accountability of *skills, knowledge,* and *attitudes* is not only for the business sector but for public and not-for-profit groups.

At this point I am convinced of the value of the hard work of using the accountability process, dealing with the complexity of describing tenable achievement-based objectives, specific content, and engaging learning tasks, of working through the accountability planner comprehensively to evaluate the learning, transfer, and impact of a program. Recently, as I taught this course with a Jubilee Associate at the University of Wisconsin, we discovered that our design had a gap: we had content on how to use a video clip, and we had a learning task using a video clip that named ways to use one effectively, but we had no specific achievement-based objective for it in our design. We addressed this gap and added an achievement-based objective: participants will have used a video clip and named ways to use one effectively. In all my experience with groups doing this course, over fifteen years, I have never seen a team in practice teaching use a video clip. But this time, two participants out of twenty used video clips in their teaching design and practice! Discovering and amending the gap made a difference.

Please do let us know how you are using this new model of evaluation for popular education in your own work. We at Jubilee will be delighted to hear from you. To the colorful principles and practices cards and seven steps of planning cards seen on the walls of Jubilee Fellows around the world, we add the accountability planner chart shown in Exhibit 7.1. with its six columns inviting use of the accountability process as each learning session is being designed. In the Introduction to Popular Education course, we shall now invite all participants to practice using the accountability planner along with the seven steps of planning.

The new Jubilee course on evaluation will be an opportunity to examine this research, see how participants have tried to apply this model to their programs through portfolio review, and move ahead on the never-ending research agenda to discover better ways to evaluate adult learning.

How do they know they know? Because they just did it to high standards they set themselves, in partnership with supportive adult educators. We have offered here a system—a model, a process, a tool—for specific measurement of adult learning. However, from all my experience, my years of working with adults all over the world, I know they know much more than any instrument can tell. We can always celebrate the kind of learning that is beyond measuring.

## EXHIBIT 7.1 THE ACCOUNTABILITY PLANNER.

| Column 1 | Column 2 | Column 3 | Column 4 | Column 5 | Column 6 |
|---|---|---|---|---|---|
| SKAs, Content, and Achievement-Based Objectives | Educational Process Elements: Learning Tasks and Materials | Anticipated Changes<br>• Learning<br>• Transfer<br>• Impact | Evidence of Change<br>• Content<br>• Process<br>• Qualitative<br>• Quantitative | Documentation of Evidence | Analysis of Evidence |

# GLOSSARY OF EDUCATIONAL, PLANNING, AND EVALUATION TERMS

This narrative glossary describes the terms used in this book as they pertain to evaluating adult learning. However, the terms about popular education found in the glossary to *Training Through Dialogue* (1995) are not repeated here.

## Accountability

(Accountable learning, accountable design.) Responsibility of the teacher for designing and teaching content such that the learner manifests the new skills, knowledge, and attitudes learned. The popular education approach stresses that the teacher is accountable to the learner; learners are accountable to one another and to themselves. This is so basic that the evaluation process presented in this book is called the accountability process.

## Accountability Process

A way of measuring the learning variable of the theory of impact (Berardinelli, 1991). It uses a simple matrix, the accountability planner, that contains the skills, knowledge, and attitudes (SKAs) to be taught; the learning tasks that help teach the SKAs; anticipated changes; expected evidence of the changes; documentation of the evidence; and analysis of the documentation. This parallels but does not repeat the planning work Jubilee teaches through the seven steps of planning.

## Achievement-Based Objectives

Popular education approach that sets objectives for the learning session that delineate exactly what learners will achieve; based on Lewin's theory that learning is most effective when it is active. This is the *what for* in the seven steps of planning. Content is embedded in the achievement-based objective (ABO). An ABO example: "By the end of this session, all participants will have examined a case study on needs assessment using four open questions and reviewed Lewin's twelve principles of adult learning." ABOs are specific and immediate, unlike goals, which are general and long-term.

## Affective

Elements in learning that signify tasks that invite learners to use their emotions, to feel the response that enhances learning. Lewin maintains that effective learning uses all three elements: cognitive (ideas), affective (feelings), and psychomotor (physical actions). Einstein is reported to have said, "We must think with the feelings in our muscles!"

## Anticipated Change

One section of the accountability planner. In the planner, there is a direct connection from the SKA being taught, to the learning tasks and materials, to the anticipated change. For example, a change in eating habits might be anticipated of people studying nutrition as a reflection of their new learning.

## Attitudes

Ways of acting that are replete with values, such as respect, openness to diverse cultures, and maintaining rigorous standards; the "A's" in SKAs. Generally caught, not taught; thus in planning nothing is more important than surrounding oneself with people who challenge one to grow. New attitudes become apparent when they are manifested in new actions or behaviors, such as when a person who was dogmatic and closed at the outset of a course becomes warmer and more open to suggestion by its end.

## Berardinelli Theory of Impact

Theory that the use of what is learned involves three variables: the learner, the experience of learning, and the workplace or environment to which the learner returns. The accountability process using the accountability planner is taught in this book as a way to evaluate the second of these, the experience of learning.

## Cognitive

The concepts or ideas being taught and learned; the "K" (knowledge) in the SKAs. The word *cognitive* comes from the Latin *cogitare,* to think. Society greatly values the thinking function; much of adult education involves passing on information, distilled concepts, and ideas. Popular education holds that all three functions—affective, cognitive, and psychomotor—work together in adult learning.

## Content

The skills, knowledge, or attitudes being taught; the *what* in the seven steps of planning. Jubilee recognizes that content is often expressed as a set of nouns or verbal nouns: for example, "how to design and use open questions"; "the difference between monologue and dialogue." Content is embedded in an achievement-based objective—for example, "participants will have distinguished between monologue and dialogue."

## Deductive

Learning tasks that move from the general or theoretical to the particular or specific. For example, the Jubilee course uses a deductive approach to teach Lewin's twelve principles; participants read and examine the twelve principles and then apply them to their own situation.

## Evaluation

A way to measure and celebrate accountability, often using evaluation instruments and reports. The purpose of evaluation is twofold: to see how much was accomplished in fact, and to examine how the design of teaching can be changed in the future. Evaluation is the consideration and reflection part of praxis: we do, we consider, we reflect, we change.

## Feedback

Immediate response to the program. Feedback is often subjective and general, offered in terms such as *I like* or *I do not like.* The Jubilee course structures feedback on practice teaching, for example, by asking the designer-teachers: What did you like about what you did here? What will you change next time? The learners, the large group, are asked: What did you like about this design and teaching? What do you suggest they (the designer-teachers) change? Feedback is not evaluation, but a step en route.

## Goal

The grand, general change that organizations or individuals expect to see as a result of education and training; called *impact* in the Berardinelli model. The Jubilee popular education course has not yet considered goals adequately; this research and this book on evaluation may help Jubilee make the goal of its entire curriculum operative from the start.

## Immediate Evaluation

A measure of the learners' responses to the design and teaching as soon as the teaching is over. It is closer to feedback than to evaluation. The four questions in the Jubilee course mentioned under the "feedback" entry in this glossary are immediate evaluation.

## Impact

What happens in an organization or to a person over time as a result of a particular educational event; the third level of the accountability planner's learning, transfer, and impact triad. How did young health educators affect the University of Washington after they learned the importance of conducting learning needs assessments? The answer, whatever it may be, reflects a program's impact.

## Indicators

Behaviors that manifest learned skills, knowledge, or attitudes. For example, a friendly response from a person that shows willingness to share resources is one indicator that the person has learned to be a cooperating member of a team.

## Individual Characteristics of Learners

One of three variables in the model of impact (see *Berardinelli Theory of Impact*). This book does not focus on it nor on the workplace variable. These may be a significant research agenda for the very near future.

## Inductive

Learning tasks that move from the particular or specific to the general or theoretical. The first learning task that reviews adult learning theory invites participants to name the best learning experience of their life, analyze it, and compare its factors to those of Malcolm Knowles; Knowles's theory is reached at the end of the learning task.

## Knowledge

One of the SKAs (skills, knowledge, and attitudes) that make up the content being taught in a course; a set of cognitive material that may be presented in a great variety of ways. In the Jubilee course, for example, selected knowledge is adult learning theory, Lewin's twelve principles, and the difference between monologue and dialogue.

## Learning

Constructed knowing, according to the precepts of popular education; skills, knowledge, and attitudes that are so internalized that they become the learner's. Such learning is available to learners and congruent with or challenging to their life experience. Learning is toward personal autonomy and supportive community.

## Learning Experience

One of the variables of the theory of impact (Berardinelli, 1991); the others are the learners and the environment to which the learners return from a learning experience. This book concentrates on the learning experience itself, especially as it occurs in the Jubilee Introduction to Popular Education course.

## Learning Tasks

Open questions put to learners along with the resources they need to respond; the *hows* in the seven steps of learning. The Jubilee course has thirty learning tasks that teach the set of content (the *whats*) that lead to achieving the objectives (the *what fors*). The teachers' role in this popular education approach is to design and set the learning tasks and be available as a resource as the students learn.

## Long-Term (Longitudinal) Evaluation

The measurement of indicators after time has passed; contrast with immediate evaluation or feedback.

## Needs and Resources Assessment

Structured process that invites learners to offer baseline data to themselves and to their teachers on what they already know about the subject being taught and what they need to know. In Jubilee this is done through the "four Ps": *picture* (take a video of yourself teaching), *preparation* (write out all the steps you take to prepare for a course), *plan* (write out your design or plan), and *perception* (invite one learner or student to respond to two questions: What do you like about [this teacher's] teaching? What do you suggest be changed?).

## Open Questions

Questions designed to evoke more than a single response; for example, "What did you like about this course?" rather than the closed question "Did you like this course?" The Jubilee philosophy is that open questions invite dialogue.

## Popular Education Approach

An approach to learning based on the assumption that human beings are the subjects of their own lives and learning, that they deserve respect, and that dialogue is an effective means of learning. Jubilee teaches people to use this approach via the course that is evaluated in this book; it stresses accountability and, in Jubilee, fifty other principles and practices that are measured in the evaluation design document demonstrated in this book.

## Praxis

Greek for *action with reflection*; a process that begins with action, invites examination of that action and reflection on it based on new knowledge, and then incites new and revised action.

## Principles and Practices of Popular Education

Guiding concepts of the philosophy, plus the techniques that move the concepts or principles into action. At this writing there are fifty such principles and practices, all of which are part of the content for the Introduction to Popular Education course taught by Jubilee.

## Program Planning

The design of learning. In Jubilee the seven steps of planning are taught to focus and catalyze this process: *why* (the situation that needs an educational intervention), *who* (those who will participate), *when* (the time frame), *where* (the site), *what* (the content), *what for* (the achievement-based objectives), and *how* (learning tasks and materials).

## Psychomotor

Elements in a learning task that call for physical action. For example, in the task distinguishing monologue from dialogue, learners are invited to put seven cards in order, then go around and examine what other table groups have done.

## Seven Steps of Planning

See *Program Planning.*

## Skills

The practices or behaviors that the learners will learn; along with knowledge and attitudes, they are part of the content of a learning-training session. Skill building has a largely psychomotor component, but is not only physical.

## Small Groups

The arrangement for dialogue used in the Jubilee approach to popular education. The dialogue is not only between teacher and learners but among learners in their small groups. The optimal size of a small group is four. The small group provides an opportunity for inclusion and safety.

## Subject as Decision Maker

View of the learner in popular education. Learners are seen as the subject of, and therefore the decision maker about, their own learning. In every learning task the open question celebrates this concept of the learner as subject. An axiom supports this: the teacher never does for the learners what they can do for themselves. Evaluators need to keep in mind that the learners are always the subjects of their own learning.

## Synthesis

A summarizing task; a way to invite learners to look back on what they have learned and sum it up. Popular education aims at a synthesis at the end of each day and at the end of the course.

## Workplace

The third model of impact variable (see *Berardinelli Theory of Impact*). It considers the quality of support a learner receives on return to the workplace or whatever site or context in which they must transfer their new skills, knowledge, or attitudes. Examining this in the light of the Jubilee mission to celebrate learning is a major research agenda.

RESOURCE B

# REVISING A COURSE WITH
# THE ACCOUNTABILITY PLANNER

## Redesigning the Introduction to Popular Education Course

In *Training Through Dialogue* (1995) we presented the Jubilee Introduction to Popular Education course as it was being offered at that time. Here we show the same course with an evaluation function developed using the accountability process and the accountability planner on all the achievement-based objectives. The course has not been radically redesigned, but now we can be more intentional and clear about why we are doing what we do. Some of the content of this Appendix appears in Chapters Three, Four, and Six; this is a compilation of that and other work done to revise the course.

As we continued through the process it became easier and easier because essentially we pasted in the achievement-based objectives and the content to the first column, then verified the learning tasks that deal directly with that content and pasted those into the second column for learning tasks and materials (what evaluation specialists call educational process elements). Documentation of evidence (column five) can come directly from the course report, which is always prepared and sent to learners. At Jubilee we are now adding a delightful and rewarding session that will complete column six; the Jubilee Associates who lead each course will conduct a session where the learners read the report together and analyze the evidence, not only to celebrate their learning but to discern places where learning did not take place. From this evidence we can make changes from course to course. A perfect praxis!

At present, the anticipated changes in learning, transfer, and impact listed in column three are very conservative. As adult educators, we know adults can respond beyond one's dreams; however, this conservative approach is appropriate as we model the accountability planner here. We will share our surprises in a journal article.

Note that evidence of change (column four) is sometimes expressed with verbs: How do they know they know? They just did it!

This appendix contains the achievement-based objectives for the present Jubilee Introduction to Popular Education course.

As you can see, this evaluation and planning process opens up many doors for both learner and teacher. At the beginning of the Jubilee course, we offer this accountability planner to adult learners as an open system, asking

- What other anticipated changes can you name for each content piece and objective?
- What other evidence can we look for here this week and later on your job?
- How can this planner guide us as we work through the week?

Remember, the key question is: How do *they* know that they know?

The work of evaluation planning need not be done alone. Invite learners to set standards from the beginning; you may be pleasantly surprised. Especially at the level of transfer and impact, learners can assert possibilities beyond your most careful plans. During the learning task about Berne's theory of communication, one nurse made it clear that her first transfer of this new skill and knowledge was going to be with her husband as soon as she got home. One can only imagine the impact of that!

In this comprehensive use of the accountability planner on the Introduction to Popular Education course, we discovered that we really had no learning task on feedback, although it is a major achievement-based objective. We shall change the course accordingly next time.

We do not show an accountability planner here for synthesis tasks such as designing together and designing to do practice teaching; these are application tasks that offer evidence of discrete learnings along the way. A more comprehensive accountability planner that puts the accountability process into full play would involve all learning tasks and all content pieces.

| Column 1 | Column 2 | Column 3 | Column 4 | Column 5 | Column 6 |
|---|---|---|---|---|---|
| SKAs, Content, and Achievement-Based Objectives | Educational Process Elements: Learning Tasks and Materials | Anticipated Changes • Learning • Transfer • Impact | Evidence of Change • Content • Process • Qualitative • Quantitative | Documentation of Evidence | Analysis of Evidence |
| 1. Reviewed current adult learning theory | *Learning Tasks 3, 11, 20*<br><br>Learning task 3: how adults learn<br><br>3A. In pairs, describe the best learning situation in your life. Then analyze it. What factors made it so good? Write these factors on SNOW cards, one on a card. We'll share all of them and then compare our factors with current research on adult learning.<br><br>Chart 3: how adults learn<br><br>*Our Factors*<br>Chart 3A: how adults learn (Knowles, 1980)<br>1. Respect<br>2. Immediacy<br>3. Relevance<br>4. 20 percent of what we hear<br>40 percent of what we see and hear<br>80 percent of what we do | *Learning*<br>Participants will<br>1. Show respect to one another<br>2. Consider immediacy of content to learners when they design<br>3. Select topics for microteaching that are relevant to this group<br>4. Design and use learning tasks so the learners do what they are learning<br><br>Participants use learning tasks to teach, demonstrating the Lewin principle that learning is more effective when it is active rather than passive.<br><br>Participants will examine teaching designs for cognitive, affective, and psychomotor aspects, demonstrating the Lewin principle. | *Learning*<br>Participants<br>1. Show respect to one another<br>2. Consider immediacy of content to learners when they design<br>3. Select topics for microteaching that are relevant to this group<br>4. Design and use learning tasks so the learners do what they are learning<br><br>Participants use learning tasks to teach, demonstrating the Lewin principle that learning is more effective when it is active rather than passive.<br><br>Participants examine teaching designs for cognitive, affective, and psychomotor aspects, demonstrating the Lewin principle. | *Learning*<br>Videotapes of the learning designs are examined to note specific examples of respect.<br><br>A videotape of a day at the course shows small groups with learners constantly engaged: observers can count the times individual speak. Records of comprehensive responses to learning tasks throughout the course show that everyone has something to offer.<br><br>The videos of the second designs note changes in the learning designs to implement feedback on learning tasks, small-group work, the need for more affective and psychomotor activity, and the need to echo and paraphrase in active listening. | *Learning*<br>These videotapes are reviewed by other teams during day five; they are sent to Jubilee for review by Jubilee Associates after the course. In those reviews we refer constantly to the four concepts: respect, immediacy, relevance, and doing.<br><br>*Transfer*<br>Jubilee does a monthly review of the designs sent in, with reports going back to participants and their supervisors showing on a five-point scale the creativity and consistency of these designs in terms of adult learning theory. |

| Column 1 | Column 2 | Column 3 | Column 4 | Column 5 | Column 6 |
|---|---|---|---|---|---|
| SKAs, Content, and Achievement-Based Objectives | Educational Process Elements: Learning Tasks and Materials | Anticipated Changes • Learning • Transfer • Impact | Evidence of Change • Content • Process • Qualitative • Quantitative | Documentation of Evidence | Analysis of Evidence |
| | Task 11: Lewin's Dozen (Johnson and Johnson, 1991) 11A. Listen to this summary of the life and work of Kurt Lewin. 11B. Each person select one number. Please read your principle for the whole group. 11C. At your table, study that single principle of Lewin; then do the practical application questions on that page with the others in your small group. 11D. Listen as all participants read their principle again in turn. What similarities do you notice among them all? Tell one way Lewin's principles will help you when you begin to design and teach. | Participants will use small groups in their teaching designs, demonstrating Lewin's principles about the power of small groups. _Transfer_ Participants use the four concepts just listed and Lewin's dozen principles as they design training on the job. _Impact_ Their organizations will begin to use these four concepts and twelve principles in meetings, training sessions, orientations, and so on. They will use this language: active learners, respect, immediacy, and relevance throughout the organization. | Participants use small groups in their teaching designs, demonstrating Lewin's principles about the power of small groups. _Transfer_ They use these four concepts and Lewin's dozen principles as they design training on the job. _Impact_ Their organizations begin to use these four concepts and twelve principles in meetings, training sessions, orientation, and so on. They use this language: active learners, respect, immediacy, and relevance throughout the organization. | _Transfer_ These designs are collected in a portfolio in chronological order and show growing use of the principles of adult learning. _Impact_ The culture of the organization changes into that of a learning, listening organization. There is a new vigor and spontaneity among employees and 30 percent less turnover. | _Impact_ The organization is celebrated as a prominent learning organization by a national review board. Its funding increases by 20 percent. Checklist for particular aspects of theory: Respect Immediacy Relevance CAP: cognitive, affective, psychomotor 80 percent do |

Task 20: Design

20A. Select one other person to make up a team of two to design and do practice teaching. Decide what you want to teach about. Select a topic that you feel strongly about. Decide whose topic will be designed and taught first.

20B. Design and do a learning needs assessment with this group on the first topic.

20C. Use the seven steps of planning and all the principles and practices to design learning tasks and problem-posing learning materials for a forty-minute session. You will design and teach for both topics together, as a team.

| Column 1 | Column 2 | Column 3 | Column 4 | Column 5 | Column 6 |
|---|---|---|---|---|---|
| SKAs, Content, and Achievement-Based Objectives | Educational Process Elements: Learning Tasks and Materials | Anticipated Changes <br> • Learning <br> • Transfer <br> • Impact | Evidence of Change <br> • Content <br> • Process <br> • Qualitative <br> • Quantitative | Documentation of Evidence | Analysis of Evidence |
| 2. Distinguished between monologue and dialogue | Learning task 6: Identify the differences between monologue and dialogue after an experience with both <br><br> 21. Design using dialogue <br><br> 25. Design using dialogue again, after receiving feedback | *Learning* <br> Participants name observed differences between monologue and dialogue. <br><br> *Transfer* <br> They design for dialogue when teaching. <br><br> *Impact* <br> Courses are consistently designed for dialogue. | *Learning* <br> They list differences between monologue and dialogue. Questions in course report about lectures as monologue. <br><br> *Transfer* <br> Designs from these participants, reviewed by Jubilee, show use of learning tasks. <br><br> *Impact* <br> Course outlines show learning tasks that invite dialogue. | *Learning* <br> List of differences <br> List of their questions in the report <br><br> *Transfer* <br> Their designs <br><br> *Impact* <br> The course plans and outlines used in their organization | *Learning* <br> The list is comprehensive in terms of their experience: practical not academic. <br><br> All questions show concern for teaching a mass of material. <br><br> *Transfer* <br> Peer review using the Jubilee checklist <br> Building a portfolio for use in the Jubilee cluster group meeting <br><br> *Impact* <br> Engaged learners sell courses, so registration numbers are up. |

| Column 1 | Column 2 | Column 3 | Column 4 | Column 5 | Column 6 |
|---|---|---|---|---|---|
| SKAs, Content, and Achievement-Based Objectives | Educational Process Elements: Learning Tasks and Materials | Anticipated Changes • Learning • Transfer • Impact | Evidence of Change • Content • Process • Qualitative • Quantitative | Documentation of Evidence | Analysis of Evidence |
| 3. Reviewed basic communications theory using the Eric Berne paradigm of transactional analysis: parent, adult, child | Learning Task 12: communications theory: parent, adult, child (Berne)<br><br>12A. Listen to this story: "My Sister."<br><br>12B. Read this brief description of Berne's theory.<br><br>12C. Listen to this illustrated lecture on Berne's theory. What are your questions?<br><br>12D. Identify verbs that you associate with any one of the ego states.<br><br>12E. In pairs, name what ego states you saw yourself in since you woke this morning. | *Learning*<br>Participants will use the language of transactional analysis in planning, working in teams, and giving feedback. | *Learning*<br>TA language use<br><br>Conflict resolution<br><br>Teamwork flows well<br><br>Action style: Participants stop and think and are quiet before speaking. | *Learning*<br>Videos of their teaching practice<br><br>Their feedback responses to the course<br><br>Anecdotes from their teamwork | *Learning*<br>Checklist of adult-adult transactions in their teaching<br><br>Their use of TA language in their feedback |

| Column 1 | Column 2 | Column 3 | Column 4 | Column 5 | Column 6 |
|---|---|---|---|---|---|
| SKAs, Content, and Achievement-Based Objectives | Educational Process Elements: Learning Tasks and Materials | Anticipated Changes • Learning • Transfer • Impact | Evidence of Change • Content • Process • Qualitative • Quantitative | Documentation of Evidence | Analysis of Evidence |
| 4. Practiced doing a learning needs assessment | Learning task 5: learning needs and resources assessment<br><br>5A. Consider the ways you saw us do a learning needs and resources assessment prior to this course: survey forms sent to Raleigh, telephone calls. What else might we have done? We'll hear all suggestions.<br><br>5B. Examine this model: study, observe, ask. Name ways this model can guide you as you do learning needs and resources assessment.<br><br>5C. Identify ways you can do a learning needs assessment in your own work situation. We'll share a sample. | *Learning*<br>Participants will use a learning needs assessment before designing their teaching practice.<br><br>*Transfer*<br>Participants will use a learning needs assessment prior to each teaching session. | *Learning*<br>Participants use a learning needs assessment and make changes in their designs as a result of doing so.<br><br>*Transfer*<br>Participants report, as in the University of Washington report in Chapter Five, that their use of the learning needs assessment has changed the quality of their teaching. | The learning needs assessment is part of their design, which goes into the course report.<br><br>Their designs, which come to Jubilee for review, include needs assessment tasks. | |

| Column 1 | Column 2 | Column 3 | Column 4 | Column 5 | Column 6 |
|---|---|---|---|---|---|
| SKAs, Content, and Achievement-Based Objectives | Educational Process Elements: Learning Tasks and Materials | Anticipated Changes<br>• Learning<br>• Transfer<br>• Impact | Evidence of Change<br>• Content<br>• Process<br>• Qualitative<br>• Quantitative | Documentation of Evidence | Analysis of Evidence |
| 7. Examined a theory of effective group work | Learning task 17 | *Learning*<br>They will use this theory in their own small-group work.<br><br>*Transfer*<br>They will use this in daily work, checking on all group and task maintenance roles.<br><br>*Impact*<br>More team planning of training | *Learning*<br>They refer to the bicycle as a metaphor for their group and task maintenance.<br><br>*Transfer*<br>Their planning is more often done in teams.<br><br>*Impact*<br>Enthusiasm, fun during planning | *Learning*<br>Anecdotes<br>Reports of how the planning went<br><br>*Transfer*<br>Team designs submitted for review<br><br>*Impact*<br>Quality of work<br>Quantity of work | *Learning*<br>Peer review<br>Self-review: how we did planning as a team, using the checklist of group and task skills<br><br>*Transfer*<br>Checklist for all roles—who did what?<br><br>*Impact*<br>Fewer conflict situations during planning |

| Column 1 | Column 2 | Column 3 | Column 4 | Column 5 | Column 6 |
|---|---|---|---|---|---|
| SKAs, Content, and Achievement-Based Objectives | Educational Process Elements: Learning Tasks and Materials | Anticipated Changes • Learning • Transfer • Impact | Evidence of Change • Content • Process • Qualitative • Quantitative | Documentation of Evidence | Analysis of Evidence |
| 8. Reviewed and used the concept of ideas, feelings, and action in learning | Learning task 7: ideas, feelings, and actions in learning Cognitive, affective, and psychomotor aspects<br><br>7A. Listen to this lecture. What are your questions?<br><br>7B. In your table groups, read this story of a nurse educator (Kate Farrell).<br><br>Using the four open questions, analyze the situation and offer suggestions for improvement (question 4). We'll share all. | *Learning*<br>Participants will name situations using these three factors as we work through the week.<br><br>Participants will design for engagement by using ideas, feelings, and actions in their learning design.<br><br>*Transfer*<br>They send designs for feedback from their workplace, asking how to include affective and psychomotor tasks. | *Learning*<br>Their designs show ideas, actions, and feelings.<br><br>They use these concepts in their feedback to one another.<br><br>*Transfer*<br>Designs sent for feedback to Jubilee<br><br>Designs in the portfolio review in the advanced course<br><br>Their questions to Jubilee | *Learning*<br>The designs<br><br>*Transfer*<br>Portfolios | |

| Column 1 | Column 2 | Column 3 | Column 4 | Column 5 | Column 6 |
|---|---|---|---|---|---|
| SKAs, Content, and Achievement-Based Objectives | Educational Process Elements: Learning Tasks and Materials | Anticipated Changes<br>• Learning<br>• Transfer<br>• Impact | Evidence of Change<br>• Content<br>• Process<br>• Qualitative<br>• Quantitative | Documentation of Evidence | Analysis of Evidence |
| 9. Identified and practiced use of the seven steps of planning | Learning task 6: monologue and dialogue<br><br>16. Designing Together<br><br>20, 24. Design | *Learning*<br>Participants will use the seven steps every time they design.<br><br>*Transfer*<br>They will use the seven steps in planning on their job.<br><br>*Impact*<br>Who: Training will be more appropriate for the selected group.<br>What, when: Trainers will not try to do too much in the allotted time so the educational potential is higher.<br>What, what for: Training is more specific and detailed.<br>How: Trainers do not rush to the *how* but are more intentional (this is both a transfer and an impact indicator). | *Learning*<br>They argue about the order of the seven steps, offering cogent reasons for their sequence.<br><br>They refer to the seven steps in the Designing Together task for the AIDS hotline. They pull out the seven steps cards to begin their planning.<br><br>*Transfer*<br>The seven steps cards are visible and the steps are used in designs shown to Jubilee for review.<br><br>*Impact*<br>Designs of training are more intentional and reasonable in terms of time, content, and continuity because the organizations are using the seven steps. | *Learning*<br>Their designs show the use of the seven steps.<br><br>Their designs show when they did *not* use a particular step.<br><br>*Transfer*<br>Those designs<br><br>*Impact*<br>Those designs<br>Meetings plans<br>Gatherings and conference designs | *Learning*<br>All steps used? Some steps omitted?<br><br>*Transfer*<br>Designs submitted from the work site to Jubilee are examined for comprehensive use of the seven steps.<br><br>*Impact*<br>Reviewed for the use of the seven steps |

| Column 1 | Column 2 | Column 3 | Column 4 | Column 5 | Column 6 |
|---|---|---|---|---|---|
| SKAs, Content, and Achievement-Based Objectives | Educational Process Elements: Learning Tasks and Materials | Anticipated Changes • Learning • Transfer • Impact | Evidence of Change • Content • Process • Qualitative • Quantitative | Documentation of Evidence | Analysis of Evidence |
| 11. Examined a video clip; identified ways to use video clips effectively | Learning task 13: using a video as a synthesis task "A Doctor Teaches Adults About Estrogen Replacement" 13A. Look at this video. Name two suggestions you might offer to this teacher in light of all you have learned so far about accountable, participative adult learning. We'll hear all. 13B. Name three guidelines for using a video clip. Listen to this lecture on ways to use video effectively. | *Learning* Participants will name a number of ways to use video, following this model. Participants will use a video in their practice teaching designs where that is appropriate. Participants will use all the criteria and guidelines they named and heard in this learning task. | Participants name a number of ways to use video, following this model. They anticipate the lecture on using video: setting a learning task first, using a video clip, replaying the focused clip. Participants use a video in their practice teaching designs where that is appropriate. Participants use all the criteria and guidelines they named and heard in this learning task. | The list of guidelines they offer in the course report Their designs using videos Videotapes of their designs using videos | |

| SKAs, Content, and Achievement-Based Objectives | Educational Process Elements: Learning Tasks and Materials | Anticipated Changes • Learning • Transfer • Impact | Evidence of Change • Content • Process • Qualitative • Quantitative | Documentation of Evidence | Analysis of Evidence |
|---|---|---|---|---|---|
| 12. Designed an effective chart and named the qualities of effective charts | Learning task 14: making effective charts<br><br>In new pairs:<br>14A. Examine all the charts we've used in this course.<br><br>14B. Name at least three criteria for an effective chart.<br><br>14C. Design and make a chart naming and illustrating your criteria. Post your chart. We'll have a gallery walk. | They will make clear and effective charts, with white space and bold printing.<br><br>They will avoid using light colors and too much material. | They produce effective charts for this task.<br><br>They produce a comprehensive set of criteria, added to by the adult educators.<br><br>The charts they make for their practice teaching use these criteria.<br><br>They offer feedback on charts using these criteria during the practice teaching. | Photographs of the gallery walk<br><br>The criteria in the course report | Compare before and after photos.<br><br>Compare charts in first and second teaching sessions. |

| SKAs, Content, and Achievement-Based Objectives | Educational Process Elements: Learning Tasks and Materials | Anticipated Changes • Learning • Transfer • Impact | Evidence of Change • Content • Process • Qualitative • Quantitative | Documentation of Evidence | Analysis of Evidence |
|---|---|---|---|---|---|
| 15. Practiced learning as subjects (decision makers) of their own learning | Learning task 3 3C. Learners as subjects (decision makers) 1. Listen to this lecture on what it means to be a subject. 2. In pairs, describe what it feels like to you to be treated like the subject (decision maker) of your own learning. Tell what this might mean to the people you work with or teach. 3. Identify one thing you have seen us do this morning to show you that we think of you as subjects of this learning. We'll share a sample. | *Learning* Participants will listen with tolerance to diverse viewpoints, honoring one another as subjects. Participants will disagree and question theory and practice, honoring themselves as subjects. *Transfer* Participants will perceive themselves and their learners as subjects—decision makers—as they design adult learning sessions. | *Learning* Participants do listen with tolerance to diverse viewpoints, honoring one another as subjects (note how many times). Participants disagree and question theory and practice, honoring themselves as subjects (note how many times). *Transfer* As evidenced in Chapter Five in the University of Washington example, participants use this language, making an effort to perceive learners as subjects of their own learning. | We (Jubilee Associates) note and record the following: The number of times the word *subject* is used The kind of response participants offer to others when they do their learning needs assessment The length of time it takes for teams to make decisions together on what to teach, and to make a design | |

| SKAs, Content, and Achievement-Based Objectives | Educational Process Elements: Learning Tasks and Materials | Anticipated Changes • Learning • Transfer • Impact | Evidence of Change • Content • Process • Qualitative • Quantitative | Documentation of Evidence | Analysis of Evidence |
|---|---|---|---|---|---|
| 16. Reviewed theory on feedback and given and received feedback | Handout on feedback to be read on Tuesday evening

Learning task 21: practice teaching and feedback

*Feedback Questions*
To the team: What did you like about your design and teaching?

To the learners: What did you like about this design and teaching?

To the team: What will you do differently?

To the learners: What suggestions do you have for changes? | *Learning*
Participants will use the feedback handout as a guide and then offer feedback as suggestions. They will accept feedback as suggestions.

*Transfer*
Participants use these feedback questions in meetings and courses.

Participants will perceive themselves and their learners as subjects—decision makers—as they design adult learning sessions. | *Learning*
Their second designs show the use of feedback suggestions.

They do not argue or defend when getting feedback, but say "Thanks for the suggestions!" | Their second designs

The feedback notes included in the course report | |

| SKAs, Content, and Achievement-Based Objectives | Educational Process Elements: Learning Tasks and Materials | Anticipated Changes • Learning • Transfer • Impact | Evidence of Change • Content • Process • Qualitative • Quantitative | Documentation of Evidence | Analysis of Evidence |
|---|---|---|---|---|---|
| 18. Examined a model for planning: the four I's<br><br>This is new content since the publication of *Training Through Dialogue.* The model is offered for your review at the end of this Appendix. | Learning task 23: a model for planning based on your first design<br><br>23A. Listen to this description of a model for planning.<br><br>23B. Examine task 12, communications theory and practice. What strikes you about the fit of this model for planning and how we did that task?<br><br>23C. Review your first design. Using SNOW cards for the tasks you designed, show how you see the model operating in your designs. Use blank cards where necessary.<br><br>23D. Name one use of this model as you go into your next design. | *Learning*<br>Participants will use this four-stage pattern when designing their second teaching practice.<br><br>*Transfer*<br>They will use this pattern when designing training at the workplace. | *Learning*<br>Their new designs reflect this four-stage process.<br><br>*Transfer*<br>Jubilee Fellows ask questions about the match of these four stages and the seven steps of planning. | Their second designs<br><br>Designs from the workplace that come into Jubilee for review (to the toll-free phone support) | Their first designs used this four-stage pattern intuitively.<br><br>The second designs show an intentional four-stage pattern. |

## THE FOUR I'S: A MODEL FOR PLANNING
## A SESSION FOR LEARNING TASK 23

| Parts | Description | Example from Berne's Theory of Communication, Task 12 |
|---|---|---|
| Inductive work | Activity connecting the content to the learner's experience. | Listen to this story. |
| Input | Research data and theory presented via charts, lists, stories, readings, lectures, audiovisual, films, and so on. | Read and review Berne's theory. |
| Implementation | Learners do something with input. | Select one situation. |
| Integration | A new activity to invite creative use of the input. | Name one use of theory in your work. |

# REFERENCES

Babbie, E. (1989). *The practice of social research*. (5th ed.). Belmont, CA: Wadsworth.

Baldwin, T. T., & Ford, J. K. (1988). Transfer of training: A review and directions for future research. *Personnel Psychology, 41*, 63–105.

Berardinelli, P. K. (1991). *Using Dubin's theory building methodology to construct a model of the impact of management training* (Doctoral dissertation, North Carolina State University, 1991). *Dissertation Abstracts International, AAI 91*, 23343.

Berardinelli, P. K., Burrow, J. L., & Dillon-Jones, L. S. (1995). Management training: An impact theory. *Human Resource Development Quarterly, 6*(1), 79–90.

Bloom, B. S. (1956). *Taxonomy of educational objectives: The classification of educational goals*. New York: D. McKay.

Cronbach, L. J. (1983). *Designing evaluations of educational and social programs*. San Francisco: Jossey-Bass.

Johnson, D. W., & Johnson, F. P. (1991). *Joining together*. (rev. ed.). Englewood Cliffs, NJ: Prentice Hall.

Kirkpatrick, D. L. (1994). *Evaluating training programs: The four levels*. San Francisco: Berrett-Koehler.

Knowles, M. (1980). *The modern practice of adult education*. (rev. ed.). New York: Cambridge Book Company.

Lincoln, Y. S., & Guba, E. G. (1985). *Naturalistic inquiry*. Newbury Park, CA: Sage.

Lofland, J., & Lofland, L. H. (1984). *Analyzing social settings: A guide to qualitative observation and analysis*. (2nd ed.). Belmont, CA: Wadsworth.

Mager, R. F. (1972). *Goal analysis*. Belmont, CA: Pitman Learning.

Merriam, S. (1988). *Case study research in education: A qualitative approach*. San Francisco: Jossey-Bass.

Patton, M. Q. (1987). *How to use qualitative methods in evaluation*. Thousand Oaks, CA: Sage.

Popham, W. J. (1988). *Educational evaluation.* (2nd ed.). Englewood Cliffs, NJ: Prentice Hall.

Popham, W. J., & Baker, E. L. (1970). *Establishing instructional goals.* Englewood Cliffs, NJ: Prentice Hall.

Rossi, P. H., & Freeman, H. E. (1989). *Evaluation: A systematic approach.* Newbury Park, CA: Sage.

Scriven, M. (1967). The methodology of evaluation. In R. W. Tyler, R. M. Gagne, & M. Scriven (Eds.), *Perspectives on curriculum evaluation: No. 1. Monograph series on curriculum evaluation, American Educational Research Association.* Chicago: Rand McNally.

Tyler, R. W. (1950). *Basic principles of curriculum and instruction.* Chicago: University of Chicago Press.

Vella, J. (1994). *Learning to listen, learning to teach.* San Francisco: Jossey-Bass.

Vella, J. (1995). *Training through dialogue: Promoting effective learning and change with adults.* San Francisco: Jossey-Bass.

Wholey, J. S., Hatry, H. P., & Newcomer, K. E. (1994). *Handbook of practical program evaluation.* San Francisco: Jossey-Bass.

# INDEX